I WAS MONTY'S DOUBLE

I WAS
MONTY'S DOUBLE

by

M. E. CLIFTON JAMES

RIDER AND COMPANY
*Hutchinson House, Stratford Place, London, W.*1
MELBOURNE SYDNEY AUCKLAND BOMBAY CAPE TOWN NEW YORK TORONTO

First published in 1954

Printed in Great Britain
by The Anchor Press, Ltd.,
Tiptree, Essex

CONTENTS

CONTENTS

CHAPTER V

MONTY AND THE CORPS DE BALLET

Page

MI 5 play dumb—A dreaded interview—The grisly hour of dawn —Waiting for Monty to appear—A curious ritual—The Gaffer and the black beret

CHAPTER VI

D-DAY DRESS REHEARSAL

The dogs of war on leash—Monty checks up—An unrecorded incident—Under suspicion—An alarming experience—A strange dog in a strange town—Awful misgivings—'The General is very pleased'

CHAPTER VII

MILITARY PICNIC IN SCOTLAND

Inquest on my first job—The next assignment—Alarming encounter with Major White—Our democratic Army—A German officer crossed the Rhine—MI 5 and Natural History—Monty in holiday mood

CHAPTER VIII

THE YEARS ROLL BACK

Meeting my terrible guardian—Dangerous adventure with the bees—A disastrous otter hunt—Arranging my future—The famous private train—Taffy the irrepressible—Monty waits for the bairns

CHAPTER IX

THE UNFORGETTABLE INTERVIEW

Surprise for a village school—'Over the top of that hill!'—Horseplay in the Highlands—Enlisting in 1914—Fred Karno's Army —Pantomime in Hyde Park—Alone with the General—'Do you feel confident?'—The real Monty

CHAPTER X

THE STRANGEST REHEARSAL ON RECORD

CHAPTER XI

A FEARFUL DILEMMA

CHAPTER XII

I MEET HITLER'S TOP AGENTS

CHAPTER XIII

FANTASTIC TALKS WITH THE GOVERNOR

CHAPTER XIV

I MEET MORE "LOYAL COLLABORATORS"

CHAPTER XV

WHAT TO DO WITH THE BODY?

CHAPTER XVI

D-DAY SETS ME FREE

CHAPTER XVII

FANTASTIC FLIGHT HOME

CHAPTER XVIII

I ESCAPE ARREST AS A DESERTER

Page

CHAPTER XIX

THE AFTERMATH

LIST OF ILLUSTRATIONS

I would never have been able to produce this book
without the wonderful help and co-operation of
Gerald Langston Day, who so gallantly came to my
rescue with his long experience in authorship

To

"EVE"

She cheered me in health, nursed me in sickness. With a courage that never faltered she refused to allow me to give up.

To her I owe my life; to her I dedicate this book.

CHAPTER I

THE GREAT ADVENTURE BEGINS

It all began one May morning in 1944 when the phone bell rang at my desk in the Royal Army Pay Corps office in Leicester.

Lifting the receiver with half my mind still on my work, I said, "Lieutenant James here." The excited voice of an A.T.S. girl operator gasped: "Oh, sir, it's a London call. You'll never guess who it is."

"Who is it, Lord Haw-Haw?"

"Oh no, sir. I was so thrilled when I heard his voice I let some of the other girls listen so they could hear him."

"Sounds marvellous. Come on, please, put him through."

There was a click. "Hullo," I said; "Lieutenant James speaking."

A pleasant voice replied: "Oh, James, this is Colonel David Niven speaking from the Army Kinematograph section. We've heard a lot about the shows you've been putting on for the troops. They're very good, I'm told. Now would you be interested in making some Army films? We've been looking round and I believe you may be the man we want."

I was stunned. Was someone pulling my leg? No, I knew that voice well and I felt certain that it was really Niven speaking to me. I heard myself saying: "Yes, sir, I most certainly should. There's nothing I should like better."

"Good," he said briskly. "Will you have a word with your C.O. and tell him I phoned you? See if you can persuade him to give you a week's unofficial leave so that you can come up to Town and have a film test. I'll send you a letter confirming the proposal. Good-bye."

Slowly I replaced the receiver. Was this an hallucination, or had the pundits who decide upon a man's job in the Army had a lapse into sanity? When war broke out in 1939 I had applied to the War Office offering to do the only work which I felt capable of doing: entertaining the troops; whereupon I was given a commission in the Pay Corps—I who could hardly do a simple sum of subtraction.

The last thing I want to do is to poke fun at the Pay Corps; I only want to show how much of a misfit I was in such a specialized department of the Army. On being posted, I embarked upon a career which was as foreign to me as Astronomy or Jungle Warfare.

"Well, James," said the Colonel when I reported to him in the orderly room, "I see you are wearing ribbons of the First World War. Be prepared for an entirely different sort of Army life this time."

I often think of the unconscious irony of these words. Had my Colonel, who was something of a martinet, guessed what a tremendous understatement he was uttering, and known the supreme annoyance he was to suffer on my account after this fateful telephone call years later, I hardly think he would have spoken so genially.

"Report to Major White's Wing," he concluded. "D.A.C. are full up, so you'd better go on Opening and Linking."

What did D.A.C. mean, I wondered as I left him, and what on earth was Opening and Linking? I found Major White in a commandeered factory packed with rough wooden tables and flooded with a brown sea of clerks who were poring over Army accounts.

The bespectacled Captain to whom I was handed over bade me a bleak 'Good morning' and stared at me as if I were a piece of flotsam.

"Bank?" he asked.

"No."

"Stock Exchange?"

"No."

"Accountant?"

"No. I'm an actor."

"Good God!" he exclaimed.

The first job he gave me was reading out a list of men's names to an elderly Private, who copied them slowly into a ledger.

"No. 31604, Private Willard," I began.

"Can you speak a bit louder, I'm rather deaf."

"*Number 31604, Private Willard. Number 72849, Private Jackson. Number 384201, Private Butler.*"

"Who-oa, not so quick," he grumbled. "This is the Army, not civvy peace-work."

I soon learned to fall into that easy-going, somnolent pace which is so characteristic of the Army. You just took everything as it came, no matter how fantastic it seemed, and trusted it would come out all right somehow.

Queer fellows gravitated to the Pay Corps. I remember one man who suffered from insomnia and who always read the Pay Regulations to put himself to sleep. Another man who was posted to us seemed incapable of adding and was so absent-minded that he once arrived in his uniform wearing a trilby hat. As we discovered later, he was a brilliant mathematician who spent his spare time working out problems in Spherical Geometry. He had risen so far above simple arithmetic that he had forgotten it.

As the months went by I was ordered to run plays and variety shows for the troops, but only in my spare time. This was a far more congenial job than adding up figures. Soldiers make very good audiences and there is none of that anxiety which oppresses an actor in civilian life—that his show may fail and that there will be no pay packet for him at the end of the week.

Presently Destiny made another move in my direction. Towards the end of 1940 a brother officer looked at me narrowly as I sat at my table and said, "You know, Jimmy, you're just like Monty."

"Monty?"

"Yes. General Montgomery, G.O.C. Fifth Corps."

"Oh," I said, and thought no more about it.

But after the sensational victories of the Desert Rats in North Africa a most peculiar thing happened. In Nottingham I went on the stage to make an announcement, and was met with loud applause which swelled into a roar. I had been mistaken for General Montgomery, the most discussed military commander in Great Britain if not in the world. The audience thought that he had come to address them.

Although taken aback, I soon forgot the incident. But some time later I took a theatrical company of Servicemen and A.T.S. to the Comedy Theatre in London and we gave a free Sunday night performance of *When Knights Were Bold*, in which years before I had appeared with Bromley Challenor. After the show a *News Chronicle* photographer came into my dressing-room.

"Excuse me," he said, "I'm told you are very much like General Montgomery." Then, giving me a critical look: "You certainly are just like him. May I take a photo?"

I borrowed a beret from someone and he took a couple of pictures, remarking that the likeness was extraordinary. But after he had gone I began to have qualms. What would happen if some High-up saw the photo of me in a beret I had no right to wear, posing as a famous General without permission? That night I dreamed that I was hauled up before the entire General Staff, numbering about 500, who sentenced me to be deported by air and dropped by parachute in Berchtesgaden.

Two days later when one of the photos appeared in the *News Chronicle* I was overcome by panic. Under my picture, looking, I must admit, very much like the General, was the caption: 'YOU'RE WRONG—IT'S LIEUT. CLIFTON JAMES.' Rather to my relief hardly anyone in the battalion noticed it.

Soon after this I was plunged into a whirlpool of work known as the Main Issue in which thousands of new allowance books had to be got ready and posted within a few days. The incident quickly passed out of my mind.

And now there had come this strange telephone call. My mind raced ahead to all sorts of exciting possibilities. But could I get away? Quite a number of people in my unit, weary of names and figures, had tried for a transfer, only to be met with a firm refusal. They were told that there was a grave shortage of trained officers in the Pay Corps and that they were playing a highly important part in the war.

One exasperated veteran who wanted a transfer to an infantry battalion refused to take no for an answer and wrote to Divisional Headquarters who also refused him. Not to be beaten he wrote to Northern Command who told him he was too old to fight. This so incensed him that he wrote to the King; but once again his request was turned down— this time by the War Office, who warned him that if he persisted he would be placed on a charge.

Remembering all this I became rather depressed; however, I went along to the Adjutant who took me in to the Colonel.

Our Colonel was rather a peppery man and a stickler for rules and regulations. He took great pride in his battalion and was very keen that it should shine in sports and competitions.

"I have just had a personal call from Army Kinematograph in London, sir," I began.

"Oh. What do they want?"

"It was Colonel David Niven who rang up."

"David Niven. Isn't he a film star?"

"Yes, sir. He wants me to go to London and help make some Army films."

"Does he, by Jove. What part of our work does he want you to film?"

I had an imaginary pre-view of a thrilling screen drama

in which a glamorous enemy spy spread alarm and confusion by vamping a pay clerk and persuading him to falsify the accounts.

"It's not exactly that, sir. Colonel Niven wants me to go up on a week's unofficial leave to undergo a film test."

The Colonel regarded me blankly. "Unofficial leave? A film test? This is a pay office, not a film studio."

"Yes, sir. He said he would be sending me an official letter confirming it," I blundered on.

"Confirming *what*?" the Colonel exploded. "I never heard of such damned cheek! Does he think he's running this battalion? If you get a letter from him, bring it straight to me."

I left his office cursing myself for having bungled the business. Once again I sat down at my desk and my roseate hopes of escaping to make films faded away. The Pay Corps was like a maze: once you were in it you could never find your way out again. As for the promised letter, I had better forget it.

But next morning the phone bell rang again and all my gloomy feelings were swept away when I heard David Niven's voice. He told me that a certain Colonel Lester in his department would be coming through Leicester on the following morning on his way North. Would I meet him at the Grand Hotel for lunch and be sure to bring along some photos of myself?

Of course I said yes. He sounded so friendly that I told him of my unfortunate interview with my C.O. the day before. To my great relief he brushed aside my fears, told me not to worry, and rang off.

It is extraordinary what power there can be in a human voice. If someone from the War Office had said the same thing in clipped, official accents I doubt if I should have been much reassured, but when Niven spoke to me my anxiety melted like the morning dew.

Next day I made my way towards the Grand Hotel feeling

distinctly nervous. Just as some grown-up men never shake
off the fear of their headmasters, so I who had been a Private
in the first war could never get rid of my feeling of awe when
meeting officers of exalted rank. I could never dissociate
them from memories of Colonels and Generals inspecting the
brilliance of my buttons and the smoothness of my cheeks.

I had this uncomfortable feeling as I stood in the lobby of
the hotel awaiting the advent of a red-tabbed Colonel with
the dilated nostrils of a man who smells something unpleasant.
But instead of this apparition I saw coming towards me, his
hand extended in greeting, a broad-shouldered man with a
close-cropped moustache, dressed in a well-worn lounge suit
and holding a battered Homburg hat.

I couldn't help liking him at sight. After introducing
himself as Colonel Lester, he led me to the bar, and over our
drinks we chatted agreeably about the war situation and my
work in staging entertainments for the Forces. During a very
good lunch I was surprised to find that he knew a great deal
about the Theatre and I quite enjoyed talking shop.

Suddenly remembering the photos, I handed them to him.
He glanced at them casually, said he thought they would do
and that Colonel Niven would be writing to me. Putting
them in his brief-case he looked at his watch and said he must
be going.

It was only after he had gone that I realized he had not
said one word about filming. What was the meaning of it?
I had spent a very agreeable hour with a most charming man,
but was that the end of my hopes? Perhaps he had formed
the opinion that I was no good for the job and had been too
polite and kind to tell me so. The next two days my depression
returned and I tried to forget it all.

But on the third morning I had an official letter from
Colonel Niven saying that I seemed to be suitable for the
post. It was very important, he said, that I should come up
to London at once and report to the address which was on

the notepaper. I was to take this letter to my C.O. without
delay and get a week's leave.

I went straight to the Colonel and handed him the letter.
As he was reading it I glanced out of the window and my
eye fell upon a poster advertising a lurid American film. I saw
a dashing young officer charging about 200 tough-looking
Japs single-handed. Good heavens, I thought, is this the sort
of thing I shall be asked to do?

The Colonel's voice brought me back to earth. "They seem
very anxious to see you," he said uncertainly. "Go along to
the Adjutant and see if he can spare you for a week. But
understand, you must be back here in exactly seven days."

The Adjutant was a friend of mine. "Sorry to worry you,
George," I said gaily. "The Colonel's given me seven days'
leave."

"Leave? What is it, Compassionate?"

"It's special leave to do a film test."

"Film test my foot!" he exclaimed angrily. "We're short-
handed, you know that."

"Sorry, old boy, it's War Office instructions." I showed
him Niven's letter. But this only made him angrier.

"Oh, these red-tabs make me sick! How can we win the
war by making films? An army marches on its pay-book."

But of course he had to make me out a railway warrant
and let me go.

I went back to my digs and told my wife the good news.
Eve was as excited as I was about this apparent 'break'. After
talking it over far into the night she decided to come up to
London with me and hear what it was all about. I put through
a call and found that both of us could stay with a friend named
David Sender who lived in Hampstead. Before the war he
had been a near neighbour of ours.

Next morning we set off in high spirits, laughing and
joking as we travelled south in the train. Although I had
worked hard I had never been much of a success in the Pay

Corps, but now I was going to do a job which I could put my heart into. In a series of dazzling imaginary pictures I saw myself as a character star, the blue-eyed boy of the Army, while my friends were still slogging away at their desks. And when the war was over I should be well and truly launched on a successful new career.

Arriving at St. Pancras, we took a taxi to the address in Curzon Street. I gave my name to the uniformed hall porter and was taken in hand by a messenger. With a cheery good-bye to Eve I followed him upstairs. David Niven was charming. We chatted for a few minutes and then he took me along a corridor to an empty room, where he asked me to wait.

It was a big room with a long table down the centre of it and with chairs arranged as if for a Board Meeting. Too nervous to sit down, I paced up and down with 'butterflies fluttering inside my stomach'.

Five minutes went by. Nobody came. I was beginning to get a little restless when the door opened and in walked Colonel Lester wearing exactly the same suit and carrying the self-same brief-case and battered hat.

He said he was glad I had managed to get away, gave me a cigarette, and then we sat down.

As he lit his own cigarette his whole manner and expression changed. In place of the charming, apparently light-hearted man I had met the week before, I was now facing a stern, rather grim-looking soldier.

"James," he said, "I'm afraid I've got rather a shock for you." He snapped his lighter shut and put it in his pocket. "You are not going to make any films."

It is extraordinary how many sinister conjectures can pass through one's mind in a few seconds. I looked at him, trembling.

To my immense relief he smiled and added: "Don't look so worried. Everything's all right. Are you patriotic?"

CHAPTER II

EVE AND THE FORBIDDEN
KNOWLEDGE

BY THE time these strange things were happening to me we had built up a mighty invasion force whose task it would be to land in France and battle its way to Berlin. It was so big and so heavily equipped that even with our superiority in the air it was quite impossible to conceal its presence from the enemy. The Germans knew where we intended to strike, but they did not know the date of the expected attack, nor could they rule out the possibility of our striking a heavy blow on some other front. So there was still some chance of deceiving them.

I believe various ingenious plans of deception were proposed by different people and discussed at a high level; but the plan which it was decided to adopt was put forward by our Deception staff and approved by General Eisenhower. It was both simple and crafty, and I think it is the first time in military history that such a plan was ever attempted.

At that time no military commander had a higher reputation than General Montgomery, and it must have been obvious to the enemy that he was to play a prominent role in the concluding stages of the war. Indeed, the Germans must have known that he would be in command of the expected invasion. The plan, then, was to produce an elaborate show of evidence that Monty had not only left his post on the South coast of England but had mysteriously appeared in quite a different part of the world.

Someone must be found who resembled him so closely and imitated his gesture and mannerisms, his gait and his voice so exactly that he would pass for the General even at close quarters. At a quick glance he must even deceive high-ranking officers of our own who had met the General. After just the right amount of discreet publicity this man would be flown abroad on an apparently badly handled tour, where enemy spies and collaborators would be allowed to see him at point-blank range and pass the information on to Berlin.

The sudden appearance of General Montgomery in Africa, or wherever it might be, would throw the Germans into confusion. What is he up to now? they would wonder. The German High Command knew well enough that he was brilliantly clever and imaginative and that he loved un-expected moves. No doubt they would think it quite possible that the cross-Channel invasion had been cancelled, at all events temporarily, and that a sudden surprise blow was about to fall on another front.

As soon as this plan was approved, top priority orders were given to our Army Intelligence department, known as MI 5, to discover a double for General Montgomery. The actual work fell on three men: Colonel Lester, who had been in Military Intelligence work all his life; Captain Stephen Watts, in civilian life a well-known dramatic critic; and Lieutenant Jack Hervey.

Colonel Lester, who was working at full pressure when the order came, at once inaugurated a world-wide search for a suitable double. Stephen Watts got in touch with a Holly-wood film star, but nothing came of this on account of his accent and the fact that he was too tall. Dozens of actors and others in Great Britain were considered, but some of them were too old, some too young, some had not the right temperament, and most of them were not sufficiently like the General.

In the Army there is no such word as 'can't'. As an old soldier replied to a recruit: "P.B.I. means Performin' the Bleedin' Impossible." But this task of finding a double for

Monty began to look so much like the impossible that even MI 5 felt a touch of gloom.

Lying in bed one night with his brain revolving round the eternal problem, Stephen Watts suddenly remembered having seen a photograph in some newspaper. It was a photo of a man in a beret with the caption: 'YOU'RE WRONG—IT'S LIEUT. ——' He couldn't remember who the lieutenant was. He couldn't even remember the name of the newspaper. But next morning he burrowed into the files of Fleet Street, identified the newspaper and discovered my name. He tracked me down through the papers of every officer called James in the British Army.

In reply to Colonel Lester's question, I told him that I certainly was patriotic. I had fought in the First World War and had been wounded on the Somme. That was why I could do no actual fighting in this war.

"Yes, yes," he said with a touch of impatience. "I know all about that. We have a complete record of your life up to date."

While I stared at him wondering if I was dreaming, he handed me a printed paper explaining that it was a copy of the Official Secrets Act.

"Read it through carefully," he said, "and when you have thoroughly grasped it, sign the declaration at the bottom."

I tried to read it, but my head was in such a whirl that the words conveyed nothing to me. For the life of me I couldn't understand what he was getting at or why I should come under the Official Secrets Act. Was I to be dropped with a cine-camera behind the enemy's lines to record some secret German activity at peril of my life? Colonel Lester seemed to me now like a Man of Mystery, one of those compelling characters in fiction who hypnotize innocent strangers into embarking upon adventures against fearful odds.

Having signed the paper I waited for the next shock. It was not long in coming.

"You know who you're like, don't you, James?"

"No, sir," I said stupidly. My brain had almost ceased to function.

"You are very much like General Montgomery, or Monty, as he is commonly called."

I was in a mood to start at shadows. It seemed to me now that I had walked into a trap. That incriminating photo of myself posing as Monty had been spotted by somebody at the War Office and I was about to be arrested and court-martialled for unlawful impersonation. Getting me to sign the paper was the preliminary to my disgrace and imprisonment.

But his next words reassured me a little. "Perhaps I owe you an apology. I have nothing to do with Army films. I am a member of MI 5, the Army Intelligence branch."

Why apologize to a man who is about to be arrested? I looked up from the carpet and met his clear grey eyes.

"You have been chosen to act as the double of General Montgomery before D-Day," he said quietly. "I am in charge of this job. It is our business to trick the enemy and perhaps save the lives of thousands of men."

The walls of the room began to sway, and his voice seemed to come from a long way off.

"Have a cigarette."

Mechanically I took one and held it to his lighter. My head began to ache and my throat felt suddenly dry. I longed for a strong cup of tea.

He said nothing for some moments; then he told me of the difficulties he had had in finding a suitable double and of his confidence that out of all the people he had contacted I was the one man who could carry out the task successfully.

He impressed on me the necessity for speed. "I have no idea of the date of the invasion, but there is no time to be lost. We shall train you to play your part, and when the time comes for you to go on the stage *you will be General Montgomery.*"

A strange feeling began to come over me, the feeling one has when a dream becomes so fantastic that common sense wakes one up.

"You will impersonate Monty in Great Britain while he himself goes abroad to launch an invasion in the Mediterranean."

As I discovered later, this was not true. It was a reversal of the actual plans which were only disclosed to me at the last possible moment. At that time they did not know if I was capable of keeping my mouth shut and so there was a double reason why they should play for safety. If, in fact, I allowed the secret to leak out, the Germans would learn the very story which MI 5 were hoping to plant in their minds. They would think that Monty was going abroad.

"Now listen carefully," the calm voice went on. "You have signed the Official Secrets Act declaration. Do you understand what this implies? You must not breathe a word of what has passed between us to any person whatsoever. While you are under my orders you will communicate with no one, do you understand? You will not be returning to your unit for some considerable time, and henceforth you must sever all connection with everyone you know. You will stay in London, and each morning at 9 a.m. sharp you will ring me at this number."

He handed me a slip of paper with a phone number written on it. "Memorize this number and destroy it. Have you any questions?"

I shook my head. Either I should have to ask several dozens of questions or none at all.

"Very well," he said briskly. "Take my advice: go to bed early and have a good sleep. Don't forget to ring me tomorrow morning."

He picked up the famous Homburg hat and pushed out one of the dents.

"By the way, we must be careful never to be seen together in public. After I have gone, wait here for a bit and then make your way out."

He put on his hat and the grim lines of his face relaxed. "I apologize for this seeming unfriendliness, but in this sort of work we often have to dispense with the courtesies."

He opened the door, but half-way out he remembered something else.

"By the way, is that your wife waiting downstairs?"

"Yes, sir."

He came back into the room and drummed his fingers on the desk. Suddenly he rapped out: "This is an order. Get rid of your wife at once. I don't care how you do it or what stories you tell her provided it isn't the truth. Understand?"

"Yes, sir."

"You'll find you won't be able to bluff her for long. Wives are usually too clever for that. Tell her—yes, tell her you're going to make some Top Secret Army films concerned with new types of armament. Get her to go back to Leicester at once."

"Very well, sir," I replied, wondering how on earth I could do it.

"Right." He went out of the door, but just before he closed it behind him he smiled and said, "Colonel Niven asks me to say he hopes you don't think him too much of a skunk."

After he had gone a reaction set in from all the excitement of the last half-hour. I don't know how long I sat in that big room letting a stream of highly coloured fancies course through my mind.

My first feeling was that I was caught in a trap, and my second was something like that nightmare I often have that I come on the stage before an immense audience and can't remember a single line of my part.

Could I really play such a tremendous role? Probably MI 5

were so desperate after failing to find someone to impersonate Monty that they were only pretending I would do. Did I look like him? I saw myself going abroad with absurd pomp and ceremony, to be greeted with roars of laughter and cat-calls from the troops, and perhaps the grim smiles of German spies, for my effrontery in daring to pose as a world-famous General. I could almost see the headlines in the newspapers when the fiasco could no longer be hushed up. I should become the laughing-stock of the world.

To think of a man like myself, who to this day has a school-boy fear of senior officers, impersonating the greatest of them all, and being saluted by Generals and Air Marshals! There was something grimly comic in the idea, but presently I began to feel a trifle better.

I thought of my Pay Corps Colonel looking at me sternly across his desk and rapping out, "Understand, you must be back here in exactly seven days." What would he do when I had not returned in seven weeks? I was involved in operations of such secrecy that it would be impossible for them to tell him the truth, and if they spun him a yarn that I was making films he would explode like a bomb.

Every actor has a role which it is his ambition to play, but whoever heard of an actor being cast to play in real life the role of a living and extremely famous General? Somehow as soon as I thought of being *cast* to play my part, the job lost some of its terror. I must look upon the whole thing as a play, and myself as the Leading Man's understudy. Of course there would be a great difference between playing a part in the theatre and playing a part in real life. Producers had always warned me not to copy the actors I understudied but to play the part in my own way. But now I should have to do exactly the opposite. I must imitate General Montgomery so closely that I *became* him.

Could I do it? Doubts assailed me afresh. And then I thought of that astonishing man Colonel Lester, and of the

STYLE AND FIT
EX-SERVICE MEN

¹ suits in 10 sizes

Political Correspondent

airmen on being demobilised are ame choice in the style and fitting as they would have in a West End

here being any austerity suits of the highest grade obtainable, nt silk linings and trimmings

s of opinion his been taken from e men So far 70 per cent of the men ference for blue suits and 20 per cent n under have chosen suits of brown or other colours

left

The demand for suits of a greenish hue is practically nil

ils

- 8 40 a m g a Cross le escape nder and n became of Newark

entered the l aguns f i eruciver f it up the per i le lent n f n has in the last

ugers was ber ware were all e mile du on carrying

isfaction of e was soon

s' claim

ation Tel lam by the or a revised cost of living on start ene ffice of th g the English

ED

and sweep uon the film e obliteration these lovely

e, while we of the long ared inhabi t us so no t us so that about una

the matter will grasp e justice the accumulation

an hour, all unday B t n is avail rriors and country who t Transport R W.

New tanks sabotaged

For M P.s to see

Types of the suits are to be shown to Members of Parliament at Olympia today For this special demonstration cubicles have been fitted with full-length mirrors

Here is a list of what the demobilised man will receive

1 left (1) 1 wide choice of shape and colours)

1 suit (1 of 8 styles in wide range of colours and over 200 patterns)

1 shirt (1 oice of 4 or 100 designs)

2 collars to m tch

1 tie (choice of over 50 designs)

2 pairs socks

1 pair shoes (black or brown),

1 raincoat (high grade yarn

Studs and links

There will be the usual number of pockets in the suits turn ups on the trousers, and legs on the waistcoat

To ensure that every soldier is properly fitted 40 sizes of each suit will be in stock at fitting out depots It is known that a range of this scope will fit more than 95 per cent of the men.

Where special fittings are needed full measurements will be taken the suit made to order and sent on by registered post.

These are the essentials of a scheme drawn up by the Ministry of Supply in collaboration with the W r Office

No details have been overlooked and a demobilised man will also receive a free stud, a back stud, a pair of cuff links and a pair of shoe laces.

Or cash

Suits will be single or double breasted If men prefer serge, and flannel's he will be able to take then instead of a suit

They will also have the option of taking a suit of £2 10s 9d in cash but the suit that a ex t is now and will to be worth £5 5s 1d in the shops

Nothing like this scheme has ever been envisaged before for t soldier on demobilisation says the Ministry of Supply when it will put being product of a m in complete on it's

Rationing
after war

Meat, fats, dairy produce

COL. J J LLEWELLIN, Food Minister said to a Conservative Committee meeting in London yesterday

When the armistice is signed you will not be able to take down loud rationing as you take down the blackout curtains In meat dairy products and fats there will uniformally be a shortage for several years ahead

Explaining the necessity for a continuance of the rationing after the war he said

You cannot take a whole lot of able young men off the farms, not only here but in Canada, the United States Australia and New Zealand deprive the land of fertilisers and transfer factory production from agricultural machinery to tanks and munitions and expect farm production to be kept up

There is going to be this period of shortage and don't let us draw back from saying it, because the important thing is to tell he people the truth

All I we are supplies in sufficient abundance to prevent their being queues before every shop we must continue with the system of rationing that has stood us in good stead

NEWS CHRONICLE

The man who brought the house down

RECOGNISE the man in picture below You're wrong His name is James Lt Clifton James producer and chief performer in the Royal Army Pay Corps Drama and Variety Group which gave its first London production at the Comedy Theatre on Sunday

Lt James finds his likeness to Gen Montgomery embarrassing "Everybody stares at me," he says.

When the Group gave a show at Leicester, the finale, a patriotic affair with Britannia as the central figure, did not go over very well.

So Lt. James donned a beret and a British warm and just walked on to the stage The astonished audience clapped and cheered for five minutes

Lt James, who comes from Perth, Australia, has been a professional actor for 25 years He made his first appearance with Fred Karno at a salary of 15s a week

Britain'
to be 1
from I

By News Chronicle

IN the first talk with t he was appointed D Overseas Airways, Brig disclosed that he is planni be the head of British pl

Gen Critchley spoke from to plan for a set of post-wa be determined

He outlined the individu and the problem of setting development of air transport within the British Common wealth.

Found a home

Despite these difficulties an others such as from internationa so air transport Critchley was ou suddenly firm that British air transport must be at least the equal of any competitor, and he was in favour of competition Controlled competition stimulated development

British Airways he sa "are without a home. We ha nowhere, in point of aircraft. We cannot hope after passengers we would like to

"If British commercial aviation is to be developed, as it should, it must have a home—an airport which will be the centre from which aircraft will radiate from Britain to the world

"The airport I find when I came into this corporation in realised that I was homeless wa to look for one I have found i

Only 12½ miles from Hyde Park Corner, there is an ideal site for an airport for London coverin 2,800 acres 1,500 acres larg than Idlewild the world's large airport now being constructed 16 miles from New York

'I am apart on these lines would be the finest advancement thi country could have I can tell you about it but I cannot tell you where it is sort'

Water runway

Detailed plans for this airpor have already been drawn meet Interesting features is that it open water or large flying-boats London is envisaged on the construction of a water runway yards long and 250 yards wide

A number of subways for the planes cross the site The principal runway is nearly 5000 yards long

The position of the site being the building of a railway line linked up with the Southern Railw to bring passengers to the platform under the British Airways bui ing at Victoria

Passengers waiting for the boat runway would be simple this part of the country woul to be found within half-mile surface Below the embank ments, Once the huge tidal excavated it would be filled natural scenery

Gen Critchley pointed althought the cost of the would be measured in million pounds, the bill would not be whatever established at this enormous sum, made available throughout

"Bluebeard" moved 27

Courtesy "News Chronicle"

WHAT STARTED IT ALL! The news story that ended M I 5's search and started Clifton James on his strange adventure From the *News Chronicle* of March 14, 1944

Photo Frank Sproston

LIEUTENANT CLIFTON JAMES, ROYAL ARMY PAY CORPS

complete confidence he seemed to have in me. How could I doubt when he was so certain that I would succeed?

And here I must say that in all my life I have met only one or two born leaders, men who cast a spell round them and infuse others with their own courage. Colonel Lester was one of them. Always quiet, unassuming, dressed in the same well-worn suit, he never wasted words but told you just what he wanted done and saw that you did it. The spell which he cast over me was so powerful that I always felt his reassuring presence even in my worst moments and when he was no longer with me.

More than once in the course of the nerve-racking ordeals which lay ahead of me I was seized with panic when thousands of miles from home. With all that terrible responsibility on my shoulders I felt horribly alone and almost at the end of my resources. And then suddenly in my mind's ear I would hear that cheery voice: "Buck up, James, you're doing jolly well. Let *me* do the worrying." And at once I would feel better.

At times he was like a father to whom I could take my troubles. At other times he was very stern and strict, like an old-fashioned headmaster. Once I was late for an appointment with him. He hated unpunctuality. I was never late again. I have always admired clever men. He was one of the cleverest men I have ever met and he had an inner strength which it is impossible to describe.

At last I pulled myself together and tottered down the stairs. Eve was sitting where I had left her. As soon as she saw me she jumped up and stared at me in dismay. As she told me later, the commissionaire seeing her sitting in the hall for nearly two hours went over to her and asked, "Are you in trouble?" When she said no, she was waiting for her husband, he remarked, "He's been up there such a time, they're either putting him on a charge or making him a General!"

"Jimmy—what's the matter? You're as white as a sheet."

She took my arm and peered anxiously into my face. I saw two of the messengers looking at us with some curiosity.

"Let's get out of this," I said. "I'm all right."

"You're not all right. What has happened? Aren't you feeling well?"

She continued plying me with questions until I was almost desperate. I replied evasively and incoherently. Full of concern, she linked her arm through mine and we went out into the street.

"Let's get a taxi," I mumbled.

The questions came at me like a stream of bullets. "Something's happened. You're in trouble. *Please* tell me."

Would she believe the lies I was about to tell her? There was hardly a dog's chance that she would.

A taxi came along and we got in. Neither of us spoke for a minute or two. I made an heroic effort.

"Listen, darling, there's nothing wrong. I am to take part in making some very important hush-hush films to do with secret armaments. I hate to say it, but I think it would be better if you went straight back to Leicester."

She looked at me sadly and her voice changed tone. "I don't believe you. I know when you're not speaking the truth. You're in some trouble. Won't you tell me what it is —and let me help you?"

I said nothing. Her eyes filled with tears and I felt simply awful. But I had to go on with it even if she knew I was lying —even if it meant a separation. I was beginning to realize how ruthless Secret Service work can be. Neither life nor death nor love must stand in the way of it when it comes to a show-down.

I knew that I couldn't stand up to her questioning for long, and so I tried different tactics. I became curt and hard, pointing out the supreme importance of the work which I had been chosen to do and explaining that if I breathed a single word to her I should have to answer for it and perhaps get into very serious trouble.

She listened to me in silence and then in a small stifled voice she said: "It's no good, you're lying to me. I suppose you want to get rid of me."

We drove to David Sender's house in a constrained silence. Eve was now convinced, as she told me later, that I had committed some military crime, while I was overwhelmed by my interview with Colonel Lester and at the same time exasperated that Eve refused to believe my story about making secret Army films.

David, thank goodness, was not only the perfect host but a naturally reticent man. Although when he saw us he must have known that something was very wrong, he asked no questions and tactfully kept up a flow of cheerful conversation. Finding that this did little to relieve the tension between us he retired to do some work in his garden.

As soon as he left us Eve laid down a fresh barrage of questions. By now I was beginning to feel worn out by the strain of what I had gone through and something like another quarrel began to develop. But after tea she went out to see her sister who lived on the far side of the Heath. I went up to our bedroom and flung myself on the bed trying in vain to think of some way to escape from this terrible estrangement which was coming between us.

I saw that I must do something pretty drastic even if it meant a complete separation and the break-up of our home. At all costs I must persuade her to leave London at once.

When she came in again I was relieved to find her much more cheerful and I hoped that our quarrel was over. We said no more about my future. Next morning at nine o'clock, feeling like a spy in a thriller, I slipped down to the phone in the hall, dialled the number and asked for the extension which I had been given. I was told to report to the War Office immediately.

Just after I had put the receiver back Eve came down and asked coldly, "Who was that you were phoning?"

As casually as I could I replied, "I was just getting my orders about this new job of mine."

"So I gathered. Who is it gives you your orders, and where is this job?"

While I was casting round for a plausible reply she put her arms round me. "Please, darling, can't you see how I'm feeling? Just put yourself in my place. There have never been any secrets between us before. Why are you so secretive all of a sudden?"

"I'm not being secretive. You don't understand."

"No, I certainly don't. You look as if you'd had a bad shock and were in dreadful trouble. Won't you tell me the truth and let me help you?"

"I have told you——"

"Yes, I know. You've told me you've been chosen to help make secret Army films. That's better than the Pay Office, isn't it? But when you came out from that interview yesterday you looked absolutely ill with worry. David has noticed it too. He asked me if there was anything seriously wrong with you."

"There's nothing wrong with me, darling."

"You never slept a wink last night and you haven't eaten anything since we came here. That isn't at all like you."

"Please, darling," I said desperately, "we can't go into that all over again. I've got to go now. The War Office want me to report at once. Stop worrying and I'll tell you what happens when I get back this evening."

She sighed resignedly, and in a sort of panic I ran away from her. My own wife had become for me the most dangerous woman in the world.

CHAPTER III

M.I.5 AS IT REALLY IS

ON MY way to the War Office I decided for the umpteenth time that the whole thing was impossible. The very idea of my impersonating a famous military commander was fantastic, and it was doubly fantastic for a man with my upbringing who had a natural fear of Colonels and Generals. From my earliest youth I had always been getting into scrapes, so that I had little self-confidence, while my fear of senior officers sprang from my childish dread of Colonel Montagu James who, on the death of my parents, had assumed the guardianship of myself, my sister and my four brothers.

My father, who was Chief Justice of Western Australia, had been a genial, humorous man, but his cousin Montagu was the living embodiment of the peppery Anglo-Indian Colonel of the 'nineties. The three maiden ladies, the Misses Hicks, who adopted us were distant cousins of his, and they used the terrible Colonel James as a bogey-man to frighten us when we were naughty.

Our 'Aunts', as we were told to call them, lived with their aged father, a retired doctor, in a rambling old house in Baldock, Hertfordshire. Fanny, the eldest, was something of a *malade imaginaire* and she spent most of her time writing sentimental short stories, not one of which to my knowledge was ever published. Milly, stout and kindly, was more interested in gardening than in children, but Kitty, the dominant one, although sharp and severe, loved us in spite of our naughtiness.

As for Dr. Hicks, who had seen the coaches go through Baldock long before the days of cars, he was one of those

senile old gentlemen who live to develop tiresome eccentrici-
ties. One of them was to go round the house of a winter's
morning putting out the fires by shovelling dead ash on to the
burning coals. Pursued by an irate Aunt Kitty he would
wave his shovel and protest in his quavering voice that he
was only tidying up the grates.

As a child I was rather frightened of him because he had
a habit of chasing me and giving voice to some ancient ditty
in Latin. If I took refuge in a tree he would wave his stick
like a baton and croak:

> Harum, scarum
> Sum divarum, etc.

or:

> Amo, amas,
> I love a lass
> For she's of the feminine gender. . . .

He had a shocking habit, too, of going out in an ancient
suit of clothes which would have disgraced a scarecrow. The
coat was threadbare, and the trousers, falling apart at the
seams, had huge unseemly patches on the seat and knees. The
Aunts never quite dared to destroy this beloved garment of
his but they buried it at the backs of drawers, whereupon the
old man would dig it up again as a dog digs up an unsavoury
bone.

Attired in his Forbidden Suit and a rusty old pair of boots,
he would sally forth to attend his only remaining patient, old
Fanny Quiver, who lived in the almshouse. On discovering
that he had gone out in this horrid garb the Aunts would
await his return with compressed lips. But knowing what was
coming to him the Doctor would bang loudly on the door
and then shuffling quickly round to the back of the house and
in through the kitchen he would gain the privacy of his own
bedroom chuckling wickedly, "Tricked them again!"

Due to the snobbery of those days we were forbidden to play with the 'common children', with the result that we were considered standoffish, and sometimes when we went out the town urchins would gather round us and shout, "Ya, ya, 'Icksie boys!" and even pelt us with filth.

One day the Aunts gave one of their tennis parties at which sedate games of tennis were combined with gossip about servants and neighbours in agreeable proportions. On the day before, my brother Charlie and I had had a fight with the ironmonger's son, who lived next door, and his rude friends. Cups delicately poised, the guests were embarking upon a stream of petty gossip. Sir Gerard Smith, late Governor of Western Australia, was there, and Phyllis Neilson-Terry, the well-known actress, at that time a girl of twelve.

Suddenly, as if by some freak of meteorology, there descended on the polite gathering a shower of dried horse dung.

After a horrified pause Aunt Kitty charged gallantly into the breach. "I am so sorry. The men are cleaning up the field over the wall. Charlie, Meyrick, run round and speak to them at once."

Charlie and I looked at each other in dismay. As we went slowly to the gate conversation was nervously resumed. Some of the visitors stood up and shook their dresses. The Aunts quickly brushed the tea table.

But a moment later the heavens discharged a still heavier downfall of manure accompanied by shouts of "Ya, ya, 'Icksie boys! Dirty ole 'Icksie boys!" And when Charlie and I opened the yard gate we were met by a raking fire of filth thrown from buckets by an enemy outpost.

Recoiling in disorder, we rejoined the main body. The guests stared in horror at our filthy condition. As for Aunt Kitty, she was furious and refused to believe that the fiasco was not entirely our fault. She sent us straight to bed with the terrible threat, "If this happens again you will go straight back to Colonel James!"

Yes, I think this imaginary picture of my guardian as a sort of military ogre must have done something to my psychology. And so too did the many boyish adventures which so often ended disastrously for me. There was for instance the first occasion when Charlie and I acted as theatrical *entrepreneurs*.

When we had nothing else to do we found endless pleasure in exploring the upper recesses of the outbuildings and unused rooms. We bored a large opening in the lath-and-plaster wall of one of the lofts and called it the Ghostly Hole. At first our imaginations peopled it with demons, ghosts and hunted criminals. But suddenly the Ghostly Hole lost all relation to its name and became a source of forbidden pleasure and profit.

One day when we had crept further along the Hole than we had been before I stumbled on a trap-door. Lifting it we found ourselves looking down into the servants' bedroom. Some time later when we cautiously returned we found the maids changing to go out. It seemed to us that our Ghostly Hole had the makings of a lucrative peep-show.

We rounded up two little boys of our acquaintance, charged them a penny for admission and made a modest profit on the First Night. We anticipated that the show would enjoy a long and profitable run, but unhappily these hopes were not fulfilled.

A few days later, having got together a full house, we crawled along to see if the strip-tease act was about to begin, when to my horror my foot slipped off the joist and went right through the ceiling of the maids' bedroom. Immediately there was an uproar. The maids in their underclothes ran screaming from their room while Charlie led the Upper Circle and Gallery in what must have been one of the swiftest retreats in history.

This struck me as most unbrotherly behaviour, for my leg was jammed tight in the hole and I couldn't move.

Presently an indignant Aunt Kitty arrived and pulled me roughly to my feet. I was packed off to bed with the terrible threat, "This time I shall *certainly* send you back to Colonel James!"

Next day no one would speak to me. Even Charlie, after blaming me for ruining our financial prospects, lapsed into a disgruntled silence. I felt sulky and depressed, but presently I was cheered by the sight of three large tins of green paint which Aunt Milly had bought to renovate the greenhouse.

All right, I thought, I'll do something which really will break this chilly silence. In the stables I took off my clothes and decorated my skin with a brilliant coat of green. Sticking a long feather in my hair and yelling like a Red Indian I rushed into the street.

Aunt Milly, sitting in the drawing-room, was conscious of some strange excitement in the road outside. People were behaving as if a lunatic had escaped from the Three Counties Asylum. Then she saw me. Swiftly opening the front door she grabbed me and dragged me into the hall.

Aunt Kitty, who by this time had come on the scene, looked at me with compressed lips. Rather to my surprise she did not send me back to Colonel James. Instead, both Aunts rolled up their sleeves and scrubbed me from head to foot in turpentine. I shall never forget the agony of that scrubbing or the painful way that my skin peeled off next day.

On arriving at the War Office I signed the form which was handed me by a messenger saying who I was and whom I wished to see, and then I sat down and waited. Many a day I was to go through this same procedure, and as time went on I came to marvel at the cheerful way these messengers did their job. People of all ages, temperaments and degrees of importance came in a never-ending stream to this nerve-centre of war. Some were calm and aloof, some vague and helpless, some excitable, some domineering and rude, but I never saw a messenger anything but polite and unruffled. Nothing seemed to disturb the placidity of these men. I wondered what they would say if I announced in impressive tones, "I am the man who is going to impersonate General Montgomery." Most probably the reply would be: "Oh yes, sir. Won't you take a seat? Looks like more rain, doesn't it?"

On this my first visit, after waiting a few minutes the messenger led me down a great many passages and at length into a room.

I don't know what most people's imaginary picture of Secret Service headquarters may be. After reading a variety of thrillers about spies and counter-espionage, I imagined a darkened room with mysterious figures wearing cloaks and false moustaches, but it turned out to be a very ordinary-looking office with an elderly woman sitting typing. She gave me a pleasant greeting and showed me into another room, where I found Colonel Lester and two officers, whom he introduced as Captain Stephen Watts and Lieutenant Jack Hervey.

At first I felt rather shy of these other two who stared hard at me for rather obvious reasons, but I soon found they were thoroughly human and lost my fear of them. The trio were a perfect team. Colonel Lester was the producer and the others were the stage director and stage manager. Both these junior officers had a thorough sense of theatre, and from the moment I met them they set to work on me with tact, patience and skill.

What I particularly liked about them was their keen sense of humour, which somehow is a thing one doesn't naturally associate with MI 5.

Time and again I would be in a panic about what might happen if I got in a jam.

"Don't be a B.F., Jimmy," one of them would say. "If some ass asks you what you're doing in the country, say you're studying Fauna and Flora. And if they ask who Fauna and Flora are, say they're two Greek Generals from Wigan."

"Suppose somebody recognizes me," I said once. "What could I do?"

"Look at him as if you were the butler when someone comes to the door and tries to sell the Duke a tooth-brush."

Of course I had to laugh, and that made me feel less nervous.

On this first morning Colonel Lester outlined the scheme. "I want you to look on this as a play we are going to produce for the benefit of the enemy. You, as a professional artiste, have been cast for the biggest role in the history of acting. Our audience are not simple, like the dramatic critics—here he looked slyly at Watts—we have to hoodwink the German High Command.

"For the next two or three days you will come here for conferences. Later on I'll arrange for you to spend a day or two on Monty's staff so that you can study his voice, gestures, mannerisms, and so on."

He threw a packet across the table. "Here are some Press photos of him."

I studied them and at once I saw that I really was rather like the General. He was an older man than I, but if I wore a beret as he invariably did I should need very little make-up. The others who had been studying me pretty closely all this time thought so too and I sensed a feeling of relief.

"I should think you'll get a good Press in Berlin," said Watts.

I began to hope so too. But I had something else on my mind. I had now been absent from my unit in Leicester for two days and if I didn't report back at the end of seven days I should probably be posted as a deserter.

When I explained this there was an uncomfortable silence. "Why not ring up and ask for an extension," Watts suggested.

I shook my head. "My Colonel would never stand for that. Even if he did, what's to happen when the extension has expired?"

"I don't know, unless we get a Double for you at Leicester."

The Colonel seemed to be lost in thought about something else, but now he came down to earth and said quietly, "I'll have a word with Pay headquarters and tell them to ring your C.O. and say you're to be released for Special Pay Duties." He grinned at me. "I don't know what Special Pay Duties means, but I suppose it means something?"

"It sounds pretty good," said Hervey."

Noticing that I still looked dubious, Colonel Lester added: "It's all right, your Colonel will do as he's told and ask no questions. Now the thing is, how are we going to get you on to Monty's staff without anyone growing suspicious and making awkward enquiries? Any suggestions, you two?"

"How about posting him to H.Q. as an official photographer?" said Stephen.

"Not bad. What do you think, James? You could follow the G.O.C. about and nobody would question you."

"There's only one thing against it, sir. I don't know the first thing about photography. What would happen if someone began talking to me about my work?"

"H'm, yes. Perhaps we'd better not risk that."

"Why not a Press reporter?" Hervey suggested.

Watts shook his head. "There aren't any Press men in on this. If it got round that a reporter was with Monty, Fleet Street would have something to say about it."

"I think I've got it," Colonel Lester said. "We'll make you a Sergeant of the Intelligence Corps. I don't think it would be unusual for an I.C. Sergeant to be attached to Monty's staff. You could mess with the other N.C.O.s and I hardly think anyone would dare ask you questions. Usually they're a bit nervous of Security people."

This plan was agreed to unanimously, and after discussing the details of how I was to be slipped into the General's staff without arousing suspicions I was told that I was free for the rest of the day.

Colonel Lester proposed that I find some cinema where they were showing a news-reel of Monty. I had little difficulty in doing so for at this time Monty was top-line news. Once again I was struck by the extraordinary likeness between us, but of course the General's whole manner was different from mine. He exuded a tremendous air of assurance which I should find it hard to imitate.

CHAPTER IV

MY FIRST REAL-LIFE ROLE

I COULDN'T enjoy the film very much because I was thinking about Eve. Just before I left him Colonel Lester had said, "By the way, have you sent your wife away?"

"She's going tomorrow, sir."

"Good." He looked at me sharply. "Did you have any trouble with her?"

"Just a little. It's all right now, I think."

As I travelled back to Hampstead in the Tube I prayed hard that I could fulfil this promise. Special Pay Duties was the latest hand-out. I hoped to God that I could put this one over on my wife and persuade her to leave London. By now I had begun to realize what a tremendous job I had undertaken. I simply had not enough energy left over to wrestle with Eve.

As soon as I got home I contorted my face into a cheerful grin and began, "Well, darling, at last I can tell you the truth."

Her face relaxed and I plunged like a Serpentine bather in mid-winter.

"You see, dear, I was approached first by Army Kinematograph section with the idea of making secret films. You know what the Army is like. Apparently they are not yet ready to go ahead. They simply wanted to get a few people lined up so that they could call on them when needed at a moment's notice. It was rather a disappointment yesterday when David Niven explained this to me and told me that the film job was somewhere in the indefinite future."

"I see."

"He went on to say that I was to report to Pay Corps H.Q. for an interview. This worried me still more. I wondered if there was some trouble about my work in Leicester. Today I went to headquarters and was told by a high-ranking officer that I was to be temporarily transferred for Special Pay Duties directly under the General's command. This will mean travelling all over the Kingdom. I may even have to go abroad."

Eve listened quietly to all this and I was just beginning to congratulate myself on having got away with it when she asked, "But what exactly does Special Pay Duties mean?"

What on earth did it mean? "Well, dear," I said at a venture, "it's a job where you go round the various commands checking up the accounts of Paymasters. It's a form of security really, something like a bank inspector checking the accounts at the different branches of a bank."

"Yes."

"So you see there's nothing to worry about, darling, and although I hate to say it I do think it would be better for both of us if you went back to Leicester. It's not as if I shall have any time to spend with you."

"All right," she said quietly, "I'll go."

I heaved a sigh of relief. At last, I thought, this wretched business is settled.

But next morning when I phoned the War Office and was told to report at once as before, I ran upstairs to say good-bye to Eve and found her sobbing her heart out on the bed.

Feeling every sort of a cad I sat beside her and tried to calm her down. At length she sat up and examined her tear-stained face in a mirror. Forcing a smile she said: "I suppose this is good-bye? Before you go I want you to know that I overheard you phoning just now. It wasn't the Pay Corps but the War Office you were speaking to. You're still telling me lies."

"You don't understand. I had to phone the War Office——"

"All I understand is that you're mixed up in something very mysterious. I won't ask you any more questions, but whatever it is you know I'll be thinking of you all the time. Will you promise me just one thing?"

"Yes, darling, of course."

"Promise you'll write to me at least once a week and tell me how you are?"

"I promise."

Only too well I knew that I should never be allowed to write a single word to her. But what else could I say?

We clung to each other for a few moments and then I left her—perhaps never to see her again.

Perhaps it was a good thing for me that I was to work at such pressure that I hardly had time to stop and think. The mills of MI 5 ground exceedingly fine. Conferences were held every day and hundreds of small details were thrashed out. There was no point however, apparently insignificant which was not gone into, and every conceivable untoward circumstance was guarded against with the utmost care.

Above everything, I was warned again and again about the need for secrecy.

"Mind you keep your mouth shut, James. Don't breathe a word to anyone. Always be on your guard. Don't trust a soul. Don't go into bars more than you can help and never drink with strangers. Be wary of anyone who accosts you. If anyone phones you, be suspicious. If someone you know asks you what you're doing in London, don't be mysterious about it but answer naturally as if you had nothing to hide. Say you're here on Special Pay Duties and refuse to go into details. If they try to pump you, give us their names and *we* will shut them up. Don't get tight. You will not write a single letter to anyone. Be careful you don't talk in your sleep."

My mind went back to 1941 when in the Pay Corps at Leicester I was hard at work on the pay sheets of men who were engaged in secret troop movements. We had been warned about keeping our mouths shut over this, but the work at this time was so arduous that there was hardly any opportunity for unguarded talking or anything else. However, when I developed a raging toothache I was at last obliged to take

MAYfair 9400/319

The War Office, A.K.1(b),
Curzon Street House,
Curzon Street,
LONDON. W.1

D.C.(D.K.) DK/K

21 April, 1944.

Dear Clifton-Jones,

Colonel Lister arrived back today and brought all
the photographs and particulars which you were kind enough to give him.

I have a part in a forthcoming production which I think would suit
you admirably. However, I must ask you to make a few tests before we
mutually decide that you and it fit each other! It would therefore be
necessary for you to come down to London for at least one week <u>as soon
as possible.</u>

In order to speed up this arrangement do you think you could
arrange with your Commanding Officer on the strength of this letter to
allow you a week's unofficial attachment here while we are making the
tests? If we ask for you officially for only one week through the
usual channels it inevitably takes about a month to arrange, by which
time the picture would be finished!!

If your C.O. would like this done through the usual channels then I
will, of course, set the creaking wheels in motion. However, the
production is of the greatest importance and urgency, and has been
ordered by the Chiefs of Staff. If the tests are successful we should
require your services for a few weeks longer, and would, of course,
make official application for the additional time.

Would you let me know as soon as possible if and for which dates
you have been able to arrange this week's absence from your unit with
your Commanding Officer.

I am writing on behalf of the Director of Army Kinematography.

Yours sincerely

Lieut. Clifton-Jones,
Army Pay Corps,
Newark Street,
LEICESTER.

Lieut. Col.
A.D.A.K.

Courtesy War Office

FILM STAR DAVID NIVEN, Lieutenant-Colonel, Army Kinematography,
writes to Clifton James In his letter, Niven offers Clifton James tests for "a
part in a forthcoming production" ("James" is misspelt "Jones")

Courtesy J Arthur Rank Organization

LIEUTENANT-COLONEL DAVID NIVEN

Photo Rex Russell

STEPHEN WATTS, critic and journalist
While serving with M I 5, he "discovered"
Clifton James for the role of "Monty's
Double"

Photo Keystone

RT HON SIR JAMES GRIGG, K C B,
Secretary of State for War, 1942-45, attended
the full-dress rehearsal of D-Day at which
Clifton James understudied "Monty"

time off to visit an Army dentist who gave me gas and extracted the troublesome molar.

When I came round from the gas, both the dentist and the doctor were looking rather solemn. At first I thought it was because there had been difficulty in the extraction, but to my astonishment they told me that I had been babbling about the destinations of some of the men whose pay-books I had been handling. Just as some delicately minded people come out with foul language when under gas, so I suppose patients with secrets on their minds are apt to talk about the very things they wish to guard most strictly.

The need for secrecy was drummed into me so persistently that at first I was scared of talking to anyone at all. But I soon realized that the last thing I must do was to give the impression that I was sitting on a secret. I must not only understudy Monty, I must learn to play another part—that of a very ordinary Lieutenant of the Pay Corps with nothing whatever on his mind.

After a few days I realized that I was very much on probation. Although MI 5 had checked up on me since my early boyhood, they could hardly afford to take any chances in such a vital plan of deception as this. For all they knew I might have developed habits and characteristics about which they had no information.

At times when I was off duty I had the uneasy suspicion that I was being followed and watched. It is a most disconcerting experience. One day I would look at some man sitting opposite me in a bus or a café and realize that his face was familiar. I had seen him before, perhaps that very morning—but where? Later on I might run across him once again, perhaps by David Sender's house. I no longer seemed to have a private life of my own.

I remember going into a bar in Shaftesbury Avenue one evening on my way home to Hampstead. A young man standing near by turned and stared at me.

"Hullo, James, fancy running across you! I don't know if you remember me? We met at a party just before the war—at Mrs. Guy Nicholl's house in Southsea."

I looked him up and down but couldn't place him at all. Certainly I had been playing at Southsea in 1939 and a Mrs. Guy Nicholl had thrown a party to which some of us actors had been invited. But I had no memory at all of this young fellow.

"What's yours?" he asked affably, and when I rather hesitantly accepted his offer he asked, "Are you on a spot of leave?"

I remembered Colonel Lester's warning not to drink or talk with strangers and I knew that my cue was to make some excuse and escape. But a spirit of perversity prompted me to stay and allow this young man to try his hand at pumping me while plying me with drinks.

At length I said: "I believe I do remember you now. At that party you were flirting with the youngest Nicholl daughter, Pat."

"I might have been," he admitted gaily.

"Smashing girl, wasn't she? Do you know where she is now?"

"I believe she's in the Wrens."

"No," I said, "you're wrong. She's in your imagination. The Nicholls never had any children." And with that I left him.

I feel pretty sure that MI 5 had put him on my track to see if he could persuade me to talk.

One morning when I phoned at the usual time I was warned that arrangements had been made for me to leave London at once. On reporting to Colonel Lester he told me the time had come for me to become an I.C. Sergeant.

"There's your stuff," he said, pointing to a full kit-bag. "You'd better try the uniform on. Don't worry if it doesn't fit you too well. I want you to look as unlike yourself as possible."

I shed my officer's uniform and got into Sergeant's battle-dress. It fitted me reasonably well and felt comfortable except for the boots.

My feet have always been tender and I hadn't worn a pair of regulation Army boots since the First World War. I felt very unhappy in them, and by way of cheering me up Colonel Lester said I looked quite unlike myself, which I can well believe.

He told me to catch the 11.0 a.m. train next morning to Portsmouth and report to a place called 'The Haven'. Nobody at Portsmouth, he explained, would know a thing about me; they would simply carry out the orders they had been given. And after I had reported I too would be given my orders.

At that time I had not yet fallen into the ways of MI 5, which were to send a man out into the blue among strangers who had no idea who he was or what he was doing. Surely, I thought, this was much too vague. I should never be able to explain myself and I should soon get into a terrible jam. And who was going to give me my orders? I should have no idea whom to ask for. It was only later that I learned to trust myself to these men who were my stage managers and who seemed never to forget anything.

Armed with a railway warrant and a permit to travel to a Protected Area, I managed to find a seat in a crowded train at Waterloo next morning. My last visit to Portsmouth had been just before the war when I was playing at the King's Theatre, Southsea. How sadly different it looked when I walked out of the station! The town had been blitzed and was nothing but a skeleton of its former self.

As I followed the deserted streets in the rain I passed rows of derelict shops with their windows out and the blinds flapping in the wind, and huge heaps of rubble where only a few years before had stood fine houses. It was nightmarish hardly to be able to find my way in a place I had known so well only a short time before.

With some difficulty I reached a desolate road with a long drive leading out of it. When I asked a soldier where The Haven was he pointed up the drive to a blackened shell of a building. "That's it, sir. Two days ago they dropped one bang on top of it. Blimey, it didn't 'arf blaze."

Rather depressed by all this I made my way to the ruin. Not a soul was in sight. Could I have come to the wrong address? Wandering round I discovered a dilapidated stable with an old-fashioned bell-pull by the door. Like Alice, I pulled it, wondering if anything would happen. The door opened, but instead of a Frog Footman I saw a smart young Corporal of the Intelligence Corps.

After he had taken my name and examined my pass, he led me down three flights of steps, and to my surprise I found myself in a huge underground building that must have housed at least a hundred I.C. personnel.

I was taken to a room where a Lieutenant-Colonel gave me a friendly welcome, after which he went out, telling me to wait. Again, like Alice, I wondered who would be the next person I should meet. The door on the far side of the room opened and a man entered wearing a dark lounge suit and carrying a brief-case and a battered Homburg hat.

"Well, James," he said, smiling, "so you found your way here all right."

By this time I was getting used to surprises. I should hardly have been astonished if Colonel Lester had come in with Mr. Churchill.

He gave me a cigarette and we sat down. "While you are here," he said, "you will meet a great many people in the different Services, and you may find that they change their ranks and regiments. One day you may see a Naval Commander, but the next time you run into him he may be a Private soldier or an Air Force ground officer. Take no notice of this. It is not your business."

I suppose I must have looked rather inquisitive, for he added: "It's a sort of chess game. Things happen on the board, but you can't see who moves the pieces about or why pawns get turned into queens."

"No, sir."

"Think what would happen if you were playing a game of chess and your chess men began to take a part in the game themselves, not knowing what was in your mind. Of course a few people have to know *something*, but the rule is that the fewest possible know the bare minimum.

"This applies to you and your little job. Hardly anyone is in the plot. I, and no one else, will tell you who these people are; but you must say nothing even to them because they know only *some* of the plot. You and I will be among the very few who know all of it."

He went on to give me my orders for the next twenty-four hours.

"You are free to do what you like until 7 p.m. Then you will change into your Sergeant's uniform. A jeep will be ready to take you to Monty's headquarters. On arriving there you will be taken to the General's Top Deception Officer. He's a very clever man, and he's in the know."

Colonel Lester smiled a wintry smile. "There is a certain rivalry between MI 5 and the 21st Army Group Deception Branch, and they would love to put one over on us. Be on your guard. He may try to catch you out."

"Yes, sir."

"You will sleep at the camp, and next morning you will be on G.H.Q. Staff. When the General appears you must shadow him; he'll be expecting you, of course. There is someone else on his staff who knows about you. Colonel Dawnay. If you get into a jam, go to him; but I don't think you will get into a jam—I have tried to guard against all possible difficulties.

"Somebody in the I.C. who doesn't know about you might grow suspicious and start asking you questions. You will be supplied with a complete set of papers made out for Sergeant James, of the Intelligence Corps. Also I have arranged for you to meet a *bona-fide* Sergeant in the Corps who is now at headquarters.

"You must question him closely about his service since the date he joined up. What were the different places where he was stationed? Who were his C.O.s and what were their nicknames? What courses has he been on? When was he promoted? And so on. Go through all this in your mind until you have memorized it perfectly, then you'll have nothing to fear if questions are suddenly fired at you."

"My memory's not too good," I said. "Suppose——"

"Suppose you take your fences when you come to them. This impersonation of an I.C. Sergeant is just nothing. Don't worry about imaginary mishaps. Worry about watching Monty so closely that you can carry a picture of him in your mind's eye."

Soon after this he left me to my own reflections, which were not very optimistic. Was I going to be another square peg in a round hole, as I had been in that first job my guardian had found for me in Cornhill?

Although nearly thirty years had gone by, I remembered with startling clearness that morning in 1914 when, dressed in striped trousers, top-hat and patent-leather shoes, a creaking old lift had carried me up to the third floor of Marsden & Co., shipping insurance agents, and with a sinking heart I had walked in through the glass-panelled door.

Before me stood a tall counter, beyond which I caught sight of several desks at which sombre-looking clerks scribbled wearily. A tall, gaunt man with a ragged black moustache came forward respectfully and took me into the office of Mr. Thomas, the Managing Director.

"Ah, James," said Mr. Thomas, rising and shaking hands. "Colonel James has told me all about you. Ah—h'm, I am sure you will be very happy with us."

I said I was sure that I would.

"It's up to you, James, it's up to you," went on my new boss, sitting back and putting the tips of his fingers together. "There is every opportunity of making good in this firm." He rang a bell and the man with the black moustache stole in obsequiously.

"Ah, Jenkinson, this is James, our new office boy. James, this is Mr. Jenkinson, our head clerk. He will instruct you in your duties."

"It will be a pleasure, sir," Mr. Jenkinson purred. But as soon as we were outside the door his expression changed as suddenly as a revue star's going off stage into the wings.

"Well, well," he said unpleasantly, "so you're the new office boy. Fancy that now. Allow me to tell you that you're the humblest member of the staff and not the Grand Duke of Cornhill. Put that top-hat away, my lad, and don't let me see it again."

Some of the junior clerks began to titter. Mr. Jenkinson, who was enjoying the scene, gave me a rapid outline of my duties.

"You will arrive 'ere at eight sharp, take out the ledgers and place them on their respective desks, fill the ink-wells, sharpen the pencils, open the mail and sort it. When the staff arrives find yourself a seat if you can and commence addressing the envelopes. I will hand you certain documents which you will reproduce on the Roneo machine, after which you will take the policies from Mr. 'Arris and convey them to their destinations as directed."

It all sounded too depressing for words and I realized that my premonitions about office life in the City were only too true.

Next morning, opening my eyes and glancing at my watch,

I found it was already the very hour at which I should be taking out the ledgers and placing them on their respective desks, etc. Dressing with extreme haste and abandoning the idea of breakfast, I tore out of the house and reached the office at a quarter past nine.

"Well, well," said Mr. Jenkinson with a sardonic grin, "fancy seein' you."

I began to say something about an alarum clock which had failed to go off, but he cut in with: "Now look here, James, when I says you're to be 'ere at eight sharp I mean eight—not nine or ten. You've upset the whole day's work. This is an office, not Madam Two Swords Exhibition."

He said a good deal more which I don't remember very clearly, gave me a packet of envelopes to address, and when this exciting job was finished, some papers which I was to deliver to the Belling Insurance Company.

Thankful for the chance to escape, I ran down the stairs into the street. In the entrance to the Belling Insurance Company's offices stood a lordly commissionaire who looked like the Duke of Plaza-toro. When I asked him where I should take the papers he was exceedingly rude.

It seemed to me that it was time someone struck a blow in defence of office boys whom everybody insulted as a matter of course.

"If the old school motto is correct," I said, "and manners make a man, you ought to be living up a tree."

He was so taken aback that he was speechless, and I marched past him feeling a little better.

Perhaps I was a little light-headed by this time, for after meeting with unhelpful treatment upstairs I lost patience, opened a large door at random and walking up to the head of the massive table at which ten or twelve elderly men sat in conclave I flung down my packet and said, "For Heaven's sake take these papers, I can't find anyone to give them to," and left the room, which had lapsed into a stupefied hush.

I sauntered back to Marsden & Co., but as soon as I entered the office there was dead silence and all eyes were turned on me. Mr. Jenkinson rose and came towards me like a hostile gunboat. "Mr. Thomas wishes to see you at once," he said.

When I entered the office marked 'Private' I found that a startling change had come over the genial Mr. Thomas.

"What is this, James?" he asked icily. "I hear that you grossly insulted Lord Belling. You had the impudence to burst in on him during a Board meeting. I have just received a telephone call from him. He threatens to break off business relations with us."

I felt very much upset about this. My boss was a most likeable man and I didn't want to cause him any trouble. I stammered an apology.

Mr. Thomas sighed and shook his head. "It's all very well to be sorry, but the harm's done."

I went out shamefacedly to be met by a caustic Mr. Jenkinson. "Well, well, well, and 'ow is Lord B.? I hope 'is Lordship will make you a co-director when you leave this establishment."

He amused himself at my expense for several days, but at length he saw that his audience was growing a little tired of his heavy sarcasm and he quietened down.

A week later I was sent to Lloyd's to deliver some policies. On my arrival there I had to line up with half a dozen other office boys, most of whom were shabbily dressed and sucking oranges.

Evidently my fame had spread abroad, for as soon as they saw me they began: "Ho, look at 'Orace! How de do, yer Lordship—I 'ope her Ladyship is keepin' well?"

I lunged out at the nearest boy and at once there was a *mêlée* which raged for several minutes until we were all thrown out by the hall porter.

When I got back to my office my suit was torn and I had

one eye half closed. Dazed and dispirited, I had no idea what had happened to the wretched policies. Mr. Jenkinson told me I was a disgrace to the City of London and would shortly be the ruin of Marsden & Co.

I didn't argue with him. Next morning I went to Mr. Thomas and told him that I had reluctantly decided that I ought to leave his employ since I was clearly not cut out to be a City magnate.

He at once agreed with a most unflattering heartiness.

"My dear James, I entirely agree with you. I am sure you are doing a wise thing in leaving us." He drew a deep breath and slowly exhaled through his nostrils. "Why, we have not had so many upsets since I joined the firm in 1871."

Generously he gave me a month's wages and I left, Mr. Jenkinson bowing me out with mock courtesy.

About six years later I was waiting to cross Piccadilly when a soberly dressed man accosted me. "Excuse me, isn't your name James? Weren't you with the firm of Marsden?"

"Yes, I was. I seem to remember your face. Were you one of the staff?"

"That's right. They're still trying to put their books straight." Tipping his hat he walked away.

This flow of memories was interrupted by a knock on the door. A middle-aged Sergeant came in.

"I was instructed to report to you, sir."

"That's right, Sergeant. Sit down. Have a cigarette."

What did he know about me? How was I to set the ball rolling without telling him too much?

Looking up from an intensive study of the floorboards I caught the suspicion of a twinkle in his eye.

"As I understand, sir, you will be going on a tricky job. If there's anything I can do to help you——"

"Thank you, Sergeant."

"I've been on some tricky jobs myself in my time."

"Have you? Well, when you're on one of those jobs I expect you have to borrow somebody else's background in case you get asked awkward questions?"

"Yes, sir."

After this it was easy. He told me that he had joined up at Winchester in April 1935, and that his first C.O. was Colonel Faraday, nicknamed Monkey Top. On the other hand, his Sergeant-Major, Edwards by name, was known as Nobby Nose. Posted to Colchester he found himself under Colonel Tucker, irreverently known as Satan . . . and so on, up to the present date.

I went through all this several times and repeated it back to him until I was word perfect. It took a surprisingly long time because he kept remembering fresh details which he thought I should know and which I had not had the acumen to ask him.

At last it was over. I shook hands with him and thanked him for his patience and help.

"That's nothing, sir," he said. "I'm only too glad to help you."

The words were commonplace enough but they didn't sound commonplace when he said them. Only those who have been on this deception work can realize quite how nerve-racking it can be. He knew from practical experience. I didn't, but I was soon to find out.

CHAPTER V

MONTY AND THE CORPS DE BALLET

WHEN the Sergeant had gone a reaction set in and instead of my previous nervousness I began to feel that if the unexpected occurred I should have no difficulty in wriggling out of it by using my wits. All these precautions, I thought, were a bit overdone. Why should such elaborate steps be taken to pass me off as a genuine I.C. Sergeant among my own people?

At this time I had not realized that wriggling out of awkward situations was not MI 5's way of going to work. These people believed in working so carefully that awkward situations never arose at all. If some avoidable element of chance remained, they would feel that their job had not been properly done.

Looking back on those days it is curious to remember the criticisms of our Intelligence Service which were so freely expressed. You heard people saying that we were always too slow and that the enemy were invariably one jump ahead of us. Why, they asked, didn't we know about the weakness of the Maginot Line or the hundreds of Fifth Columnists in Europe? Why were we in ignorance that Hitler was going to attack Norway or invade Crete? What on earth was our Secret Service up to not to know years before that Hitler was building up a mighty army to sweep through Europe?

If we could see the secret reports which were sent in by our agents we should probably realize that they did know these things, and as to justifying their reputation for astuteness and foresight, they are always obliged to remain silent. I met only a few of these men and I took part in only a very small part of the vast plan of deception for which they were responsible, but even this was enough to convince me that I was dealing

44

with people who were at least as clever as their opposite numbers in any other country.

After my talk with the Sergeant I was glad to escape into the open air and cool my brain. Presently I drifted into a café and tried to eat something, but I had no appetite. So I went to a cinema, but instead of the news-reel of Monty which I hoped to see I was treated to one of those third-rate musicals with the comedian dressed as a city 'slicker' and surrounded by a bevy of South Sea Island beauties flashing their pearly teeth and wriggling their hips. This was the civilization we were fighting for. I tried to follow the story, but constantly heard the words, "Keep your mouth shut! Be on your guard!" mixed up with "Colchester, Monkey Top and Nobby Nose". I have often noticed that in real life the ludicrous is mixed up with the grim, just as it is in Nature.

By seven o'clock I was back at headquarters dressed as an I.C. Sergeant, and when I reported, the Lieutenant-Colonel told me that my jeep had arrived. He took leave of me with the usual rather ominous "Good-bye—and good luck." As I walked out of the building no one seemed at all surprised that I had arrived as an officer and was leaving as an N.C.O.

It was dark outside and raining. A young Captain loomed up from the gloom and said: "Hullo, Sergeant, all fit? Let's get cracking, shall we?"

I saluted and climbed into the jeep with my tooth-brush and razor rattling in the pocket of my battle-dress. This was my first experience of that famous Army vehicle. The Captain, who obviously was thoroughly at home in it, drove it like a shell along the rain-swept roads. Having no overcoat I soon began to feel cold and wet, and my forage cap kept slipping over my left eye.

Turning abruptly off the main road into a narrow lane, we jolted across a field and came to a stop in a wood where I could dimly see rows of tents with some Nissen huts in the centre. The Captain led me to a tent standing apart from the others and told me to wait. In the semi-darkness I could see a thin palliasse with a couple of Army blankets, my bed for the night.

Presently the Captain returned with the news that the Colonel would see me at once. Rather nervously I followed him to one of the Nissen huts for my dreaded interview with the Top Deception Officer. Although the hour was late I could see dozens of officers sitting at tables, all hard at work.

The Colonel was young and handsome, but with the tired, strained look of a man who has long been working at top pressure without a break. He gave me a searching look before speaking.

"You will spend tomorrow with General Montgomery. You know your orders? Take your place naturally as a Sergeant of the Intelligence Corps on Staff Headquarters. If you should find yourself in difficulties, report to Colonel Dawnay and no one else, understand?"

"Yes, sir."

He seemed about to dismiss me, but suddenly he rapped out, "Where did you do your training?"

It is extraordinary how disconcerting such a question can be, fired at you like a pistol shot, even when you have been expecting it. For a moment my mind went blank. Just in time I recovered myself.

"At Winchester, sir, under Colonel Faraday."

"Show me your AB 64."

"Yes, sir." I handed him my pay-book.

He glanced at it quickly and gave it me back. "Right. That's all for now. A jeep will pick you up tomorrow night."

He paused for a moment and stared fixedly at me. I waited for the inevitable "Good luck, James". When it came I saluted and left the room.

Back in my tent a dark feeling of uncertainty oppressed me. This Top Deception Officer was a man whose opinion really did count. Why had he stared at me in that curious way?

Of course he wanted to see for himself whether I looked like Monty, but what was his verdict? It seemed to me that he was more than a little doubtful about my looks.

The more I thought about it the more worried I became. At last, unable to stand it any longer, I went back to the hut and asked an officer I had not seen before if I could see the Colonel again. For some reason he looked almost scared and pointed silently to the door as if unable to speak.

I knocked and went in. The Colonel looked up with a frown. "Yes, what is it?"

"You know why I'm here, sir," I burst out. "Do you honestly think I am like General Montgomery?"

For the first time since I had seen him his face relaxed. He almost smiled.

"You've no need to worry, James, the likeness is extraordinary. When you came into the office the first time, my men outside thought it was the G.O.C. on one of his surprise visits. Whoever chose you for the job knows what he's doing."

I left him feeling very much relieved.

Alone in my tent I thankfully took off my boots, lay down on the palliasse with both blankets drawn over me and lit a cigarette.

This striking resemblance of mine to the G.O.C. was a curious thing. When you come to think of it, the world goes almost entirely by outside appearances. If a man looks like a saint it is easy for him to be a crook because people trust him, whereas if he looks like a crook he can behave like a saint but he will never readily be trusted. Here was I looking so exactly like General Montgomery that even men who saw him every day mistook me for him. And yet I knew that our characters were completely different.

The son of a Bishop and brought up in Tasmania, Monty had developed a strong character of his own before he was ten years old. He had inherited his mother's will, and in playing with other children he was passionately eager to be the leader.

Impatient of all restraint, he would get into trouble by challenging other children to dangerous feats of daring.

When the family came to England and Bernard Montgomery was sent to St. Paul's School, Hammersmith, he plunged with ardour into every sort of game and within three years he was Captain of the First Eleven at cricket and of the First Fifteen at rugger. Not only did he want to excel at games, he wanted to command. It was much the same with his career. Against his parents' wishes he chose the Army instead of the Church. From the first he felt himself a born leader of men.

My own background was entirely different. I had never wanted to lead anybody, and to the horror of my guardian I had chosen to go on the Stage. I had no natural authority or gift of organization. I could never have become a General in a thousand years.

Full of such thoughts I lay awake throughout the night and was just dropping off to sleep in the small hours when I heard a voice outside.

"Are you there, Sergeant?"

I pulled open the tent flaps and in the dim light of dawn I made out the figure of a Private who handed me a bowl of cold water, a mug of cold tea, a thick slice of bread and marge and a little piece of burnt bacon.

Although I managed to shave in the dark, I couldn't face this repast. A quick, icy splash, a rub down with my pocket handkerchief, and I was ready.

Ten minutes later I was off in the jeep again with the young Captain. We sped along for twelve miles or so, then turned into a drive leading up to a fine old country house standing in its own grounds. In the grey light I could see a line of cars and jeeps drawn up on one side of the forecourt, with their drivers standing talking in low tones. The column was headed by a Rolls-Royce flying General Montgomery's pennant.

We got out and the Captain went inside to report. Soon he

came out again, got into his jeep, and with a "See you tonight, Sergeant," he drove off.

I began to feel horribly ill at ease and self-conscious. Some of the drivers had stopped talking and were obviously discussing me. What was my next move? I couldn't just stand there as if I didn't belong.

Becoming aware of a very tall figure striding towards me, I looked up, and saluted a Colonel of the Guards.

Speaking in a low tone he said: "I am Colonel Dawnay. If you're in any difficulties, report to me. Stay as near the General as you can without attracting too much attention. Go in that car," he pointed to a Humber, "and sit in front with the driver. Understand?"

"Yes, sir."

I went over to the car. Behind me I heard quick footsteps and an irritable voice, "Are you the photographer?"

Turning round I beheld an angry-looking Captain coming towards me like a trough of low depression.

"You standing there," he roared, "are you bloody well deaf? I'm asking if you're the photographer."

This was my first test that morning and I'm afraid I didn't come out of it very well. Having had no sleep and practically nothing to eat since midday the day before, I felt quite as irritable as the Captain.

"No, I'm *not* the photographer," I said testily, and turned my back on him.

He shot round in front of me with surprising agility for a man of his build. "Say *sir* when you speak to an officer. Get into that car."

Pulling myself together I saluted and got in. The driver gave me a sly grin. " 'E's all right, Sarge. Bit of a bastard sometimes, but he don't mean any 'arm."

By now the light was stronger. Without warning the Rolls glided forward and stopped outside the main entrance to the mansion. My driver at once moved up to just five yards behind

E

Monty's car. I glanced through the back window of our Humber and saw the whole line of vehicles moving into place, each one exactly five yards behind the car in front. As I learned later, this was the strict rule of procedure. Whether the cars were stationary or moving, the five-yard interval must be rigidly preserved.

I remember once a car for some unknown reason dropped a few yards behind its proper position. At once a precise voice called out: "Stop. What's the matter with that fourth car? See to it, please."

One of the General's aides hurried to the offending driver and dressed him down. Not until the formation was properly adjusted did Monty give the order to move on again.

Switching off his engine, my driver got out and stood by his car, and I noticed that all the other drivers had done the same. Evidently this was part of the drill. I scrambled out and stood by my driver.

Five minutes passed. There was an unmistakable tension in the air. Then suddenly there began what was known as the Corps de Ballet, a set performance which took place every morning when the General made his first appearance. The timing was exact, and it was played as carefully as any theatrical show.

First the Colonel came out with the two aides, whereupon Monty's chauffeur, a Sergeant, called us to attention and saluted. The Colonel and the aides walked slowly down the line of cars and then the Colonel went back into the house.

At this point we all silently counted six, after which, on the tick, the Colonel reappeared with a Brigadier. Up and down the two of them walked, and then the Brigadier made his exit.

Then we counted twelve, and on the twelfth count the door opened and out came Monty with the Brigadier. He gave us a quick look round and a brief smile before returning the Colonel's salute. As far as I know, this curious performance never varied from day to day by a single movement or by a fraction of a second.

This, of course, was my first view of the Corps de Ballet, and I watched the General like a hawk. At once I noticed that he had a special salute of his own—a slight double movement of his hand which made it more of a greeting than an official military salute.

I had thought so much about him, read so much about him, heard so much about him that now he was here before me in the flesh I was more than a little excited. Wearing the famous black beret, and over his battle-dress a leather, fleece-lined flying jacket, he looked exactly as I had imagined him. To all appearances he was 100 per cent fit and without a care in the world. When it suddenly came home to me that this was the man I had got to *be*, some of my elation at seeing him began to evaporate. Could I ever look so full of health and quiet confidence?

For a few moments he stood talking to the Brigadier and Colonel Dawnay. Then the door opened again and out came a civilian whom I recognized from Press photos I had seen of him as Sir James Grigg, the Secretary of State for War. With the Brigadier and Grigg, Monty got into his Rolls and off we went.

We kept our regulation five yards behind the Rolls and my eyes were glued on the General. I noticed that he sat in the left-hand seat, and through the back window of his car I tried hard to notice his gestures as he talked to the War Minister.

We sped along the country roads. Not many people were about at this early hour, but the few we passed stopped and stared. Then suddenly recognizing the famous black beret they would grin and wave wildly, receiving in return that friendly salute.

Monty missed no one. Once we had just passed through a village and I saw standing by a hedge an old farm labourer, his eyes fixed on the approaching procession. As we drew level with him, Monty gave him a smile and a salute. The old chap looked a bit taken aback, and then suddenly he recognized the General.

Being just behind, I saw the expression on his old, weather-beaten face. It was unforgettable. In a flash all the horror of the past few years, the bewilderment at our reverses and the apprehensions for the future were swept away. Here was the man who would lead us to victory: Monty, the man in whom every man, woman and child was placing his trust for the coming invasion. Taking off his battered hat the old man slowly waved it and his eyes filled with tears. It was so moving that it left in my mind an impression which will never fade.

CHAPTER VI

D-DAY REHEARSAL

WE TURNED off the main road and came in sight of the sea. As we drew up near the beach the scene was extraordinary. I had known I was to attend a full-dress rehearsal of D-Day, but I hardly expected the marvellous spectacle which met my eyes that cold May morning.

Off-shore as far as the eye could reach were battleships, cruisers, destroyers and other ships of all kinds. Huge tank-landing craft were disgorging tanks, armoured cars and guns by the hundred. Overhead the air was thick with planes, while infantry poured ashore from invasion barges and rapidly moved inland.

Over on the right stood a big unoccupied hotel with a flat roof where all the Chiefs of Allied Command were standing watching the operation. Monty, with Sir James Grigg, got out of his car and went to join them. For a moment I wondered if I should follow him, but I decided to wait until he came back to the beach.

In about a quarter of an hour he reappeared, and at once a small procession formed behind him—the Brigadier, Colonel Dawnay, with the two aides, one of whom was the irate Captain who had taken me for a photographer. I slipped into place behind them, uneasily conscious of the stares of military policemen who must have wondered who was this nondescript I.C. Sergeant who had suddenly appeared on the scene. It seemed incredible that I was here on Monty's staff to see the dress rehearsal of the greatest invasion in history.

Once again I was overwhelmed by that feeling of unreality which sometimes comes in dreams. This time I was caught up in one of those nightmares in which you are swept along irresistibly to some hideous climax such as finding yourself in a completely false position. When I looked at this mighty armada it was quite absurd that I could expect to pass for the man who was in charge of it, and I began to get stage-fright.

When first you take up acting and suffer from this unpleasant malady you imagine it is a beginner's complaint, but as the years go by you come to realize that it is a chronic disease. It may even get worse. No matter how well you know your part or how thoroughly the show is rehearsed, when the curtain goes up on the first night you are terrified.

This was the feeling that swept over me as I took my place among these men who had been right through the African campaign with Monty. And besides this, I felt like a jackal among lions, a masquerader among heroes who had earned the right to be in attendance on this famous General. At that moment I heartily wished that I had never met Colonel Lester and that I was back in Leicester sedately copying out the details of soldiers' pay accounts.

But as I looked at the busy scene on the beach I reflected that perhaps one month hence many of these men would be severely wounded or dead. I remembered the Dieppe raid and how the enemy were sitting waiting for it. And the thought came to me, if I played my part successfully thousands of these doomed men would escape. I might be a 'phoney' with no right to pose as a veteran of the African campaign, but what did this matter if I did not fluff my part when it came to the real thing?

Monty moved off, talking rapidly to the men beside him. I followed, and my stage-fright left me. The pace increased so that I had difficulty in keeping up with them, but as I watched Monty I forgot everything else. He strode along dominating the scene, but never interfering unnecessarily. Every now and then he stopped and fired questions at officers, N.C.O.s and Privates—checking up, offering advice, issuing orders, and all the time I kept my eyes fastened on him.

What personality he had! On the stage I have seen even rank bad actors and singers get away with it because they had personality, and I have seen really competent artistes without personality who could get nowhere at all. This man was what we should call a 'natural'. The moment he appeared, before even he spoke, his personality hit people bang between the eyes.

He would have made a fortune on the stage, I thought. Here in this great war drama he had carefully chosen his cast, appointed the cleverest directors, managers, technicians and property men, and from the leads down to the walk-on people he was making certain that every one knew his part.

By now the invasion scene was approaching its climax. The sky was even blacker with aircraft and the infantry were plodding up the beaches in still greater numbers. It looked to me as if many of them had been cooped up in the landing craft for days and that some of them were still feeling seasick. Monty's dislike of sickness either in himself or in others was so well known that they tried valiantly not to show it, but in spite of their efforts quite a number of them looked a sickly grey and they reeled slightly as they came along.

I was watching Monty and at the same time trying to take all this in, when he became the centre of one of those homely incidents which are so characteristic of the man.

Within a few yards of where I was standing, a very young soldier still looking seasick from his voyage came struggling along gamely trying to keep up with his comrades in front. I could imagine that, feeling as he did, his rifle and equipment must have been like ton weights. His heavy boots dragged in the sand, but I could see that he was fighting hard to conceal his distress.

Just when he got level with us he tripped up and fell flat on his face. Half sobbing he heaved himself up and began to march off dazedly in the wrong direction.

Monty went straight up to him and with a quick, friendly

smile turned him round. "This way, sonny. You're doing well —very well. But don't lose touch with the chap in front of you."

He put his hand on the boy's shoulder and carefully adjusted his pack which had slipped.

When the youngster realized who it was that had given him this friendly help, his expression of dumb adoration was a study. Such incidents made me understand how different real life drama is even from the best synthetic drama as portrayed on the Stage.

I thought how great a change must have come over the Army in the last thirty years. All the time I was in the trenches during the First World War I never once set eyes on a General. In fact, the only time I saw one at all was in 1914 when hundreds of us were paraded on Salisbury Plain. An elderly gentleman resplendent in gold braid trotted quickly down the line on his horse, hardly looking at anyone, and obviously thinking of his lunch.

At half-past twelve Monty made his way back to his car, and I sensed a general feeling of relief that things had gone fairly smoothly. By this time I was absolutely famished, but I had heard so many stories about the well-known Monty Austerity that I was beginning to wonder if on these strenuous occasions anyone had any lunch at all. I was relieved when the watchful Colonel Dawnay appeared discreetly beside me and said, "You will go in that jeep," pointing to one which was drawn up with the cars.

When I got into it the driver grinned at me and said impudently: "Wotcher, Sarge. Have those b——s fagged you out?"

"No, they haven't. It's these boots that are crippling me." I bent down and loosened the laces, experiencing the relief of a heretic when Torquemada and his crew loosened the thumb-screw.

The driver persisted, "What I meant was—anything wrong?"

"No. Why should there be?"

He gave me a knowing look. "No offence. Just wondered."

I saw that he was suspicious of me. It wasn't surprising. These drivers on Monty's staff had probably been together for years and they knew one another well. Then all of a sudden an unknown and rather green-looking I.C. Sergeant appeared among them. Who was he? What was he up to?

"When there are a lot of Brass-hats about they usually send one of us along to keep an eye on things," I said cryptically. It meant about as much as a Minister hedging on an awkward question in the House of Commons, but to my relief it shut him up.

All the same, I still felt uneasy about this conversation. If I was to spend some weeks with these men I must allay any doubts they had about me. As soon as possible I must contrive to get on a friendly footing with them all.

The procession set off, but at various battalion, brigade and divisional headquarters Monty and the War Minister stopped for a discussion while the rest of us kept at a respectful distance. Monty would ask for certain officers he knew and talk to them quietly and informally, going through the details of the morning's work. He seemed to have a grasp of every minute particular, and a way of impressing his wishes on all and sundry, which made it impossible for anyone to forget.

As he said years later, when addressing a gathering of eminent men at the Mansion House: "If you tell the soldier what you want, and you launch him properly into battle, he will always do *his* part—he has never let the side down. Never. The British soldier is easy to lead; he is very willing to be led; and he responds at once to leadership."

I remember him saying: "I know. Do it my way. This is what you will do." Again and again I heard these words.

Most of the officers were young men. Many of them had never yet been under fire, and they were facing one of the greatest battles in history. Inevitably they must have been

feeling nervous about it. And then along came this man who
inspired them with such a magical degree of confidence that
you could see their fears melting like the morning mists.

I began to see that the Army on active service was not
really so unlike the theatrical profession. Many a time I have
seen a cast stale, tired and dispirited after weeks of hard
rehearsing. Everyone who has been on the Stage knows that
'dead spot' which comes some little time before the First Night
when it seems a foregone conclusion that the show will flop
and you will be out of work again, going the weary round of
agents. And sometimes I have seen a producer come in, grasp
the situation at a glance, and with a few quiet words change
the whole atmosphere so that everyone was cheerful and
confident again.

Monty did just this. I had read about great Generals in
history who made speeches to their men on the eve of battle
and infused them with a fighting spirit which won the day.
Now I saw this actually happening. Monty did not get on to
a rostrum and shout an oration through a battery of loud-
speakers; he spoke quietly, man to man, and it was far more
effective. I saw, too, that a man who is capable of inspiring
his subordinates like this and leading them to victory must of
necessity be ruthless.

It was obvious that he would tolerate no second-rate
performers in his 'cast', and I noticed his habit of turning
suddenly on a man and fixing him with those piercing eyes
of his as if he could read his innermost thoughts. It seemed to
me that this electric stare had the effect of keying men up to
a higher pitch of intensity and that the General himself was
at such a high pitch that he could sense when others were
too far below it.

The strain of watching him, coupled with hunger and
fatigue, began to tell on me and I allowed my attention to
wander. Suddenly I was conscious that Monty had stopped
talking. In the dead silence I looked up and saw those piercing

eyes fixed on myself! It was a strange and rather alarming experience. I felt like a very small boy caught out in some misdemeanour. Time seemed to stop and I almost sank into the ground. Then Monty looked away and went on talking.

At half-past one the cars turned into a field where there was a group of camouflaged huts and tents under some trees. This was a divisional headquarters. Monty and his entourage got out and made their way to the officers' mess.

On the right was a mobile kitchen, and I lined up with a long queue of drivers, signallers and others who were waiting to be served. After the cook had dumped a helping of stew into my mess-tin I made my way towards a group of drivers who were sitting on fallen tree-trunks having their lunch. As I neared them, conversation ceased abruptly and they all looked at me with suspicion.

I felt very much like a strange dog which has been set down in an unfamiliar neighbourhood and has got to get on a friendly footing with the local canine population. What is it that passes from dog to dog when these animals use their noses to establish relations? Probably some subtle radiation unknown to science. I tried to radiate a feeling of friendliness to these drivers, and presently we were conversing amiably about Brass-hats. Most Privates and N.C.O.s have no very high opinion of 'Brass', and so I took the line that *somebody* had to keep an eye on them because they were too busy with matters of high military importance to look after themselves.

By the end of lunch they were almost friendly, though still obviously on their guard. An hour later we were off again on our tour of inspection in the pouring rain, until five o'clock, when we set off for G.H.Q.

There was no ceremony about the General's exit. After he had disappeared into the house with Sir James Grigg, the curtain was down and I began to realize how bone-tired I was.

I was whirled back to I.C. headquarters in the jeep, and when I had changed back into my uniform I caught a night train to London.

For nine hours I had followed Monty round and I felt confident that I could imitate his voice, gestures and mannerisms, but his personality was quite a different matter. It was so unique and overpowering that I despaired of ever *being* him. It was one thing to ape the outside of a man, but quite another to acquire something of his fire and forcefulness. When he stopped and spoke to people they felt something which came from inside him. What would they feel if *I* stopped and spoke to them? Nothing at all. I would seem like some miserable tailor's dummy dressed up in the likeness of a popular hero.

What I needed was a transfusion of morale such as sales managers of furniture firms attempt to give their unfortunate travelling salesmen who have to sell their goods on H.P.

I thought of the salesman's job I had once had with the firm of Pendragon, when unemployment on the Stage was at its height, and of the Salesmen's Hymn which we had been forced to sing in the morning:

> Play the good old game,
> Pendragon is the name;
>   We'll do our best and never fear the worst.
> When selling's tough we'll grin
> And take it on the chin.
>   Rah, rah! we'll get our quota by the First!

'First' referred to the first of the month, by which date we were expected to have sold our quota of £50-worth of the firm's rather dubious furniture.

It seemed to me, too, that my background was so utterly different from Monty's that I should never be able to bridge the gulf between us.

While I was a schoolboy at Aldenham, he was a Lieutenant

in the Warwicks and had already been to India. The limit of my own travels then since early childhood was West Runton in Norfolk, where the Aunts invariably took us for our holidays.

Five years after the end of the First World War, Major Montgomery was teaching young officers military tactics. At that time I was the Marshal of France in a tour of that famous old drama, *Under Two Flags*, but in the words of the Frenchman, *"C'est magnifique, mais ce n'est pas la guerre."*

And so it went on until the Second World War came. Major-General Montgomery was in command of the Third Division and I was a Lieutenant in the Pay Corps.

No, I couldn't go through with the part. I should have to convince Colonel Lester that I wouldn't do and persuade him to find someone else while there was yet time.

I was still in this frame of mind when I awoke next morning, and on my way to the War Office I rehearsed in my mind what I should say to make my 'producer' see reason. Things were now more like Alice through the Looking-glass: everything was happening the reverse way round. For in normal life you try to cover up your deficiencies and bluff your way through, but now I must exaggerate my shortcomings and do my best to get the sack.

When I was shown into the familiar room Colonel Lester gave me a very peculiar look.

Drawing a deep breath I tried to take the plunge. "Good morning, sir. . . . I'm sorry, but——"

"Sit down," he interrupted. "Have a cigarette."

This rather put me off my stroke. While I was lighting up he said: "Before you tell me anything about being sorry I want to tell *you* something. The General is pleased, very pleased, with the way you did your job yesterday."

I was surprised and shaken, but I made another attempt.

"Look, sir, I want you to——"

"Yes, yes, I know how you feel. Yesterday was a bad

dream. The part is too big for you. You think you'll never be able to carry it off. Well, you're wrong."

For the first time since I had met him he showed signs of emotion. Standing up he fixed me with his eyes, and the thought crossed my mind that all these forceful men who have to deal with subordinates in ticklish situations use their eyes hypnotically.

Leaning over the table towards me his voice came at me like a pistol shot. "Can't you get it into your thick head that you are going to be a smash hit? Do you think I'd have taken you on unless I was certain of this? Are you going to back out when you have it in your power to save the lives of thousands of men?"

The hard lines of his face relaxed and in a different tone he went on: "Perhaps you haven't taken in what I told you just now. *General Montgomery is very pleased with the way you did your job yesterday.*"

"Yes, sir, but——"

"But what?"

"When it comes to the real thing——"

"When it comes to the real thing you'll sail through it. Don't keep imagining. Before you went down to Portsmouth you imagined all sorts of things, didn't you? But you got through splendidly. It will be the same when we come to the real show. Just take things as they come, and for God's sake leave the worrying to me."

CHAPTER VII

MILITARY PICNIC IN SCOTLAND

WHEN I remembered this scene later I realized what a clever man I was dealing with. The whole essence of cleverness in handling human problems is knowing the way people are going to act and react. Really it is a process of getting inside their minds. Whether you are a doctor or a politician, a barrister, a General or a publicity manager, you will get nowhere unless you have this gift of tapping people's thoughts and feelings.

Colonel Lester certainly had this gift. He knew almost exactly how I had felt the day before and what I should be likely to say when I met him again. What is more, he knew just how to meet this situation and pump courage and confidence into the deflated balloon. When I came to think of it, he was hardly likely to let me go after the arduous experience he had had in finding a double.

In a very short time I was myself again, and I heard myself saying: "It was a wonderful show yesterday, sir. I wish you had been there to see it."

"I was," he replied casually.

I stared at him in astonishment and noticed a twinkle in his eye.

"I saw the whole thing," he said. "Once I was standing quite near you but you didn't see me."

"You don't mean—disguised as one of the drivers?"

He evaded the question by asking me one: "Well, what do you think of it all now? Did you come up against any snags?"

I told him about the drivers, how they seemed to resent having a strange I.C. Sergeant come amongst them.

He shook his head. "Nothing to worry about. It's quite natural for them to be on their guard. What else?"

"I forgot to say 'sir' to one of the Staff Captains. He was very angry and yelled at me."

"Good. That adds a bit of verisimilitude. It might have been better still if he had put you on a charge."

I looked at him and saw that he was laughing.

"That was about the only thing that went wrong, except that once when I let my attention wander I came to and found the General staring at me."

"He's psychic," said Colonel Lester, and I knew just what he meant. '

"Give me a little more time," I said, "and I think I can impersonate Monty as far as his gestures and mannerisms go. If he were slow and stolid it would be much more difficult, but he's so quick and has so many unusual mannerisms that I think I can take him off all right. But I wasn't always near enough to hear what he was saying. I should have to study him at closer quarters before I could imitate his voice."

"Good. This is just about what I expected. We shall have to arrange to get you closer to him. Report here on Tuesday next at 4.20 in the afternoon and be ready for a week's trip. I'll tell you more when I see you."

I took it easy for the next day or two, got into mufti and tried to relax.

One afternoon I had been to a cinema and was returning by Underground. At the lift I had to show my ticket, and I had just extracted it from my wallet when looking up I found myself face to face with Major White of the Pay Corps. Turning quickly I stuffed my wallet into my breast pocket and hurried away. To my dismay a voice shouted "Hey!" I doubled round a corner and found myself at the foot of the circular stairs.

I don't know if you have ever tried running up the stairway of an Underground station. Long before I had got half-way up I was panting like a fish out of water, goaded into superhuman efforts by the voice behind me, which was shouting at me to stop. At last I came to a halt and a wave of anger passed through me at my being pursued in this way by the officious Major. But in a few moments a little man in a bowler hat came up the stairs holding out my wallet, which in my haste I had pushed between my coat and my waistcoat!

When I returned on the Tuesday I found Jack Hervey in the office with Colonel Lester. The plan, I heard, was for Hervey and myself to go up to Scotland where General Montgomery and a few of his Staff were spending a week's holiday. As an I.C. Sergeant I should accompany him wherever he went, and to end up with I should have a private interview with Monty so that I could get hold of his voice exactly and study him at point-blank range. This time I was to stay with Jack Hervey in comfort at a nearby hotel.

He concluded by saying: "Time is short. Can you finish your study of the General in a week?"

It was hardly a question, it was an order; but I was able to reply with some confidence that a week would be enough for me.

In the days when Mr. Hore-Belisha was War Minister I remember reading that the British Army had been made democratic. With the idea of encouraging the recruiting drive, I suppose, the notion was put about that even Privates had a royal time of it and were treated very much like officers. I remembered this with a certain bitterness as I walked with Jack Hervey to the Tube station staggering under the weight of a full kit-bag, while he dangled an elegant officer's hold-all.

"Look here," I said, dumping my kit-bag on the pavement, "can't we have a taxi?"

"Pack up your troubles," he replied with an irritating grin. "The Treasury draws the line at Sergeants joy-riding in taxis."

"Well, damn it, you might take a turn yourself with this ruddy thing."

F

"We mustn't spoil you, Jimmy. This is a toughening-up course."

At Euston station it was even worse. While he sauntered to his first-class compartment and sleeper, I was left to battle for a third-class seat among a milling crowd of Other Ranks.

In the night my compartment, which was packed tight with tars, many of whom were also "tight," gradually discharged itself until I was left with a solitary sailor stretched out on the seat opposite me. We talked about the war, and to my astonishment he began to give me a detailed account of the Navy's work during the D-Day rehearsal.

I tried to stop him, but with the persistence of a Scot he insisted on disclosing war secrets which I felt sure the Germans would have given a lot to get hold of. Had I been a spy I should have had an easy and profitable night's work.

The train slowed down for Perth, and as he was getting ready to leave me I couldn't help saying that I thought him rather incautious to open his mouth to a complete stranger.

His answer was disconcerting. "Och, mon," he said, "if I canna tell one of you Security chaps, who *can* I tell—Churchill?"

Early in the morning I got out at Inverness with a throat like a third-class waiting-room and my head feeling like a lumpy flock mattress, to be greeted by Hervey, rosy and cheerful after a good night's sleep. But I felt better after a wash and some breakfast, and our drive out of Inverness through some of Scotland's loveliest scenery was as good as a tonic.

Our driver, an R.A.S.C. man who knew Jack well, told us that Monty's special train was drawn up by a siding at a little place called Dalwhinnie. He had orders to report there in the evening, so that we could take our time and have lunch on the way.

The countryside was very different from England's. Mile after mile we travelled without seeing even a village, but in the early afternoon we came to a small inn whose doors and windows were bolted.

After Jack had banged away on the door for some time it was opened cautiously on a chain and the frightened face of an old woman peered at us through the aperture. At length she seemed satisfied with our looks and let us in.

"I thocht ye was furriners, likely," she said.

"Honest Jack Hervey of Hervey Hall," Jack replied with a low bow. "As true-blooded an Englishman as ever wore the King's uniform."

"Och, we get all sorts in these pairts," said the old woman, leading us to a comfortable dining-room. And she began telling us about the foreign troops stationed in the neighbourhood who were as wild as March hares and always trying to get at her daughter, so that she had to keep the doors and windows bolted. But she knew a gentleman when she saw one. Janet would wait on *us*.

I thought of that ancient war ditty, 'A German Officer Crossed the Rhine', and imagined a beautiful girl with lily-white skin and golden hair. It was rather a shock when the door opened and a muscular, raw-boned woman of forty strode in with a large tray. Surely her mother's precautions were a trifle overdone?

We got to Dalwhinnie at about four o'clock and as we came down the hill into the village I saw a file of great mountains receding into the far distance with here and there the gleam of silver-grey lochs which lapped their feet. For a few moments I was overcome by the peace and quietness of a land which had never been seared by a modern war or sullied by industrialization. And then my eye fell upon a train of six coaches standing just outside the station, and I knew that I was looking at the brain and nerve-centre of an impending invasion which meant terror, destruction and death.

We drove to the small hotel, fixed up our rooms and had a (for those days) unbelievable tea of ham, tongue, fresh home-made scones and cakes, a large bowl of fruit and a pint of thick cream. Jack went off to report and left me to my own reflections.

The pace was beginning to quicken now. At first I had been sent on a mere trip to Portsmouth. Now I was up in the North of Scotland. In a fortnight I should be—where? I had no choice, no knowledge, of where I should go. Like a kite I was being dragged along on a quickly lengthening string. Soon I should rise aloft, resplendent in the uniform of a full-blown General.

Jack came back to say that I was to report to the train at nine o'clock next morning when Colonel Dawnay would give me my orders. He strongly suspected that arrangements had already been made for me to meet the great man alone. I had already been warned about this but none the less the news came as a shock. He shot me a quick glance and suggested that we explore the mountain which towered above the hotel at the back.

I was thankful for something to take my mind off what lay before me and we set off on a stiff climb. Soon I was puffing and blowing, but Jack with his enthusiasm for natural history seemed tireless.

"Now, Jimmy," he would say, "about two hundred yards in front of us there is a patch of scrub. Do you see it? I'll circle to the right and you go round to the left. I think we'll find a ptarmigan's nest."

"How on earth do you know that?"

"I saw the cock bird chasing the hen back on to her nest. They often do that when the hen's sitting."

Sure enough we did find a ptarmigan's nest. We also found a golden plover's. Soon I became thoroughly interested, and it would have been a very unimpressionable man who could not lose himself in the marvellous view we had from the mountain-top.

On our way down again Jack went on talking about birds

and flowers. What should I have thought in April if someone had told me that in a month's time I should be in the Scottish Highlands while an MI 5 officer talked to me about wild life to keep me from worrying?

That night as I lay in bed thinking things over, my position seemed to be more unreal than ever. Although a commissioned officer I was now masquerading as a Sergeant—a Sergeant with no duties to perform except to watch a General who to all outward appearances needed no watching or guarding. Although a complete outsider to the other N.C.O.s, who were a close fraternity, I had to mix with them and get along with them as best I could. They were very curious about me and a single unguarded word or action might spell disaster.

The same thing applied to my dealings with the officers on H.Q. Staff who must have wondered who on earth I was. Although an officer myself, I must remember to salute even the most junior of them and to jump to any orders they gave me. I was nervous about making a slip, being put on a charge by one of these officers and finding myself obliged to ask for help. If this happened I felt sure that Monty would be greatly annoyed at my clumsiness.

Then again, my orders were to follow the General very closely from moment to moment and from day to day. Seeing that Monty was on a holiday away from all military cares and responsibilities this was likely to arouse suspicions in the minds of people who were not in the know. When I was shadowing him during the D-Day rehearsals it was not so difficult: it was natural for him to have a Security Sergeant on his Staff. But here in this remote Scottish village surrounded by officers and men who had become his own personal friends I must have seemed absurdly *de trop*.

When I took my place among the drivers on that first morning in Dalwhinnie I found myself in a kind of *opéra bouffe*. These men seemed to know every detail of their officers' habits and mannerisms, and even of their private lives, and of course they had a nickname for each one of them. Standing by their cars waiting to move off for the day's picnic, they were up to all kinds of schoolboy pranks which they would break off instantly whenever an officer hove into view.

It was rather like being back at school again. Monty was the headmaster and his officers were the form masters. The Sergeant driver was the prefect trying to keep order in the classroom while waiting for the master to arrive for the morning's lesson.

On this first morning a batman came along and began loading up the cars and jeeps with picnic baskets.

One of the drivers, Bill by name, exclaimed: "Wotcha, Alf, what's 'is Lordship takin' for dinner? Roast duck and champagne?"

"Don't be so iggerant, Bill," another driver remarked. "The nobs don't 'ave champagne, they drink hock."

"That's what that piece in the pub says when I tried to date her up," put in another driver. " 'Hock I,' she says."

Bill took a clod of grass from the bank behind him and was about to throw it when the Sergeant driver barked, "Look out, lads." In a moment they were all standing at ease beside their cars as a Lieutenant came up to the train.

As soon as he was gone, Bill picked up the clod, hurled it at the driver who had spoken, missed him and hit an inoffensive batman. Pretending that this was his target, he turned to the others and said, " 'Ow's that for a beauty?"

"Bull's-eye," said somebody.

"Boss-eye," said the driver he had missed.

In spite of their boisterous behaviour they all thought the world of their officers and they simply worshipped Monty who was in a genial, holiday mood. I think he knew quite well the way his men behaved behind his back—and he welcomed it.

"It has been said that the British are the happiest soldiers in the world," he said in a speech when receiving the Freedom of the City of London in 1946. "They appear to carry about with them an inward cheerfulness which makes them able to laugh at discomfort and make a mockery of danger. Of all soldiers the British are the best humoured. And this is equally so when they are hard pressed and when conditions are adverse. Private soldiers out on patrol in No Man's Land have often been heard to mutter asides, and strengthen each other with ribald jests. The inexhaustible wit of the soldier—and in particular of the Cockney—is one of our most valuable possessions."

He certainly lived up to this dictum himself. He smiled and joked with his Staff, took a keen interest in the details of each day's excursion even to the extent of having good-natured arguments about how to keep the food fresh and the tea or coffee piping hot.

At meals he never monopolized the conversation. He was just a genial master on an outing with some of his boys. He chatted gaily about birds, beasts and flowers and quietly pulled his officers' legs if he found them ignorant of natural history. The war seemed to be far away. I don't remember hearing him refer to it once.

As to his energy, it was astounding. Often he would order the cars to halt. Jumping out he would take off his jacket, flex his arms, take deep breaths of the invigorating air, and then set off down the road at a good swinging pace, all the time talking in an animated way to those who were with him. It is possible that he was discussing military strategy at times, but I don't think so. I believe he had deliberately pushed the war out of his mind and forgotten it.

The more I studied him, the harder I found it to believe that this dapper, soft-spoken man was to lead our great armies into Hitler's European fortress. There he would stand, smiling at some remark of his youngest officer as if the great battle before him had already been won.

In his own mind no doubt it had. The whole thing had been planned with such care and precision that there only remained the comparatively routine business of putting it into effect. And since for the moment there was nothing further to be done, what could be more sensible than to retire to Scotland for a week's fishing and picnicking?

The only thing which reminded me of warfare was the military precision with which even the picnics were planned and carried out. The cars had to be at the exact five-yards interval and everything in apple-pie order before Monty made his début in the morning. No one seemed to hurry, but each man had his job to perform with the greatest efficiency and exactitude, whether it was cleaning and tuning a car engine or packing a picnic basket. I realized how a single man of genius could so impress himself on his subordinates that everything they said, did and felt was, as it were, a part of his character. From what I saw of Monty the last thing he did was to slave-drive his officers and men. He inspired them with a desire to drive themselves.

It has always astonished me how such fanciful and derogatory stories about him should have been put about. Only the other day I met an ex-officer who had served under his command.

"Monty!" he snapped, when the conversation got round to him. "I disliked the man intensely. A swaggering braggart. He used to terrify his officers on principle."

"Did you ever meet him?" I asked.

"Oh no, but I heard all about him."

I prefer to remember the frail old lady, a complete stranger, who came up to me on the sea front.

"Excuse me, sir, but you were Monty's Double, weren't you?"

When I admitted it she laid her hand on my arm. "He is a wonderful man. My son was one of his soldiers. When he was killed I wrote to the General about him and he wrote back. Now he sends me a letter every Christmas. My boy would have been so proud to know this."

She shook my hand and slowly walked away. I saw that Monty had brought great consolation to that old lady and that it was all done in secret.

CHAPTER VIII

THE YEARS ROLL BACK

ON THE following day we set off together towards the train, Jack chattering away on all sorts of topics. But now I scarcely listened to him. All I could think about was the coming interview with Monty, and the more I thought about it the more nervous I grew. My ancient fear of senior officers had come upon me with redoubled force.

The years rolled back and I was a boy of sixteen just having left school, on my way down to Honiton in Devon, where I was to meet my guardian, the Terrible Colonel James. He was going to decide my future.

The last time I had met him I was only two years old, so that I had no memory of him. With long, sleek hair brushed straight back, and a brightly coloured tie to match an equally bright pair of socks, I was no doubt dressed in very bad taste, but I enjoyed the train journey, fancying myself a smart man of the world.

These delusions of grandeur were soon dispelled when I reached Honiton station. There, waiting for me, watch in hand as if he were ready to tick me off for coming late on parade, was a short, dapper man with sharp grey eyes and a well-trimmed military moustache.

I went up to him, but before I could speak he barked out: "So you're Meyrick? The first thing you can do, my boy, is to get your hair cut!"

A governess cart was waiting outside the station. As we drove off I ventured, "A nice-looking pony, sir."

Colonel James merely stared at me. "Get those damned socks off," he said. "Dreadful colour."

As we drove along the country lanes he frequently took

74

...s hat and nodded to the people we met. His close-cropped hair was pure white, contrasting strangely with the big blue patch of skin high up on his forehead. Every time he removed his hat I could not help glancing at it.

"What the devil are you staring at?" he queried sharply. Without waiting for a reply, he added, "If you want to know, I've been stung."

"Stung, sir?"

"Yes, sir, stung. By my favourite bee, Roger."

Good heavens, I thought, is the old man crazy? But when we arrived at our destination, a lovely old house standing in its own grounds, I saw a row of bee-hives at the bottom of the garden; and before I was even allowed to unpack he told me that this was Honey Collecting Day and that I was to assist him in this task, which I soon saw he intended to carry out in the manner of a military operation.

"Wait outside," he ordered, and presently he appeared from the house wearing a long coat, a straw hat and veil, leather gauntlets and top boots. I, of course, had no defensive armour at all.

The Colonel marched briskly down to the hives, and gave me the Order of the Day.

"Now, sir, when I say 'Tops off', whip off the tops of the hives smartly."

I stood there nervously, wondering how many bee stings it took to kill a man.

"Are you ready?"

I nodded uncertainly.

"Right! Tops off!"

I advanced at the double, lifted the tops off two of the hives, and then retreated in disorder as two angry swarms rose into the air. Standing his ground, the Colonel puffed smoke at them from a large smoke-gun, and then to my amazement he shouted orders at the bees as if they were a pack of hounds.

"Tommy, Tommy, steady, my boy! Back, Ernest, back, sir! Down, Jacky, get down!"

He turned round to me. "Don't stand there like a fool. Get the honey out, man."

Somehow I managed to do as I was told, and after receiving only one sting I heard the welcome order to retreat.

I fancy he wanted to test my mettle, and I was just congratulating myself on having come through the ordeal not too badly when I was dismayed to hear that I was expected to go otter hunting with him on the following day. He told me this at dinner, an uncomfortable meal during which he asked me searching questions about my progress at school until I managed to divert the conversation to his military exploits in the field.

Next day I rose unwillingly at dawn and left the house most unsuitably dressed in my new town suit and thin shoes. The Colonel had already gone on ahead.

Arriving at the rendezvous in a village four miles away, I saw a crowd of red-faced men in knickerbockers and big boots and horsy-looking women with strident voices. Each of them carried a long pole, and as I approached them they stared at me as if they doubted that I was British.

Presently one of them blew a loud blast on his horn and off started the hunt at a good swinging pace, leaving me standing there in my urban finery, an object of wonderment to the village children. There was nothing for it but to follow at a jog-trot. I have always had tender feet and I had not gone a quarter of a mile before my tight shoes began to hurt me. Along with some stragglers I left the road and plodded across a sodden ploughed field. We jumped ditches, scrambled through hedges and climbed over five-barred gates. Soon I was so far behind that I lost contact with the last of the laggards.

Feeling a keen and increasing sympathy for otters, I made

my way back to the main road and walked slowly along it until I came to a little country inn. Inside it I sank into a chair, undid my shoes and buried my face in a large, cool ginger beer. Some little time later I wandered back to the house, rehearsing the conversation I should have with the Colonel when he returned home.

"I did go otter hunting, sir, but most unfortunately I lost touch with the hunt. A stone got into my shoe and by the time I had taken it out there was no one in sight."

But for some reason my guardian, who I believe had never gone to the hunt at all, came back late that night, by which time I was in bed, and next morning at breakfast he merely bade me a curt good morning and retired behind *The Times*. Concluding his silent meal, he stood up, brusquely bade me report to his study as soon as convenient and marched out of the dining-room.

When I reported he said stiffly: "I understand that you failed to keep up with the hunt yesterday. You slacked about, sir, and were seen entering a public house."

After this he told me that he had arranged for me to go as an office boy to the firm of Marsden in Cornhill at ten shillings a week.

"You are very lucky to have such a fine start in life," he said with a touch of complacency at his own cleverness.

Jack Hervey had stopped talking. "What's the matter with you?" he asked sharply. "You're getting the wind up again. Is it about your meeting with Monty?"

"Well, yes, I suppose it is."

"What's there to be afraid of? He's not like the Grand Cham of Tartary who has the Executioner standing behind him in case you make a slip."

"No, I know."

"What's the trouble, then? It's only the little men who are difficult to get on with, the nobodies who stand on their dignity. The big men are dead easy—unless you've got across them, which you haven't."

We walked on again.

"Do you know the story of Napoleon and the Swedish recruit?" Jack went on. "Whenever Napoleon saw a man he didn't recognize he always fired three questions at him in the same order: 'How old are you? How long have you been serving? Did you serve in either of my last two campaigns?'

"Not being able to speak French, the Swede was coached by his pals in the correct replies, but when Napoleon spotted him, for once he put his questions in the wrong order.

" 'How long have you been serving?' he asked. The Swede replied, 'Twenty-three years.' '*Tiens!*' exclaimed Napoleon, 'how old are you?' 'Three years, sir.' '*Sacré Tonnerre!*' cried Napoleon, 'either you are mad or I am.' 'Both,' said the Swede."

Of course I had to laugh, and by the time we reached the train I was in quite good form.

The station was very small and neat with a beautifully kept garden on each side of the line, a tiny booking-office and two small cottages housing the station staff and their families. About one hundred·yards from the end of the platform was the goods siding, and there I saw Monty's famous private train. It consisted of two thirty-foot covered trucks for the cars, a luggage truck, and four corridor coaches converted into a self-contained headquarters, with offices, messrooms, kitchens and sleeping quarters.

At intervals military policemen stood on guard, and all the cars with their drivers were drawn up beside the train with the General's Rolls in front. I noticed that as we approached everyone stopped talking.

After Jack had reported, Colonel Dawnay came out and gave me my orders. It sounded to me a curious mixture between a military parade and a spree. Most days, he said, we should be having a picnic lunch. I was to travel in a jeep as before and mess with the drivers.

I found the same irrepressible driver, whose name was Taffy, sitting at the wheel of the jeep.

" 'Ullo, Sarge," he began. "How are yer? Come along to keep an eye on things?"

At this moment the Captain and the other aide came bustling along followed by several batmen carrying hampers, which they packed into the jeeps. A third officer also appeared, and as I looked at the three of them I was struck by the peculiar way they were dressed. Ever since I had held a commission I had been under the shadow of strict discipline regarding dress, and I imagined that on H.Q. Staff the discipline would be even stricter. Yet here were officers wearing battle-dress blouses, suède shoes and corduroy slacks of many colours.

Then I noticed an even more peculiar thing. One of the aides entered a compartment and when he came out again his blouse was bulging in front.

Taffy caught my eye and said in a low voice: "You ain't seen nuthin' yet, Sarge. He's a lad, that one."

The officer sidled along to the jeep like a broody hen, took a quick look round, then slid what looked like a bottle out of his blouse behind one of the hampers, tucked a rug round it and turned away.

It may, of course, have been an innocent soft drink, but Taffy grinned and exclaimed in a hoarse whisper, "Strewf, if the ole man catches him wiv that lot he'll get the order of the W.C. and Chain."

The whole thing began to strike me as a comic opera. Would they have the Corps de Ballet before the picnic? Sure enough the performance soon began: it was carried out with the same faultless precision as when I had seen it before.

When Monty appeared on the count of twelve I understood why his Staff wore coloured corduroys. Their Chief was similarly dressed with a grey roll-top sweater and of course the black beret. He gave us all a quick smile, chatted about the day's arrangements and got into his car. We all got in too. The engines started up, but instead of moving off the procession remained immobile.

I saw Monty glance up at the windows of the two cottages by the station, and presently several small children and some women appeared up above and began to cheer and wave small Union Jacks. Monty at once waved back at them with a gay smile, and gave the word to move off.

Some people might have taken this for the act of a show-man, of a man who loved publicity, but it did not seem like this to me. Monty is genuinely fond of children and he did not wish to disappoint the little Scottish boys and girls who cheered so shrilly from the windows. He knew they wanted to see him go, and so he waited until *they* were ready.

It was a charming gesture from a great soldier.

CHAPTER IX

THE UNFORGETTABLE INTERVIEW

THE procession set off with Monty and the Brigadier in the Rolls and the precise five-yards interval between each pair of cars. Passing through some of the most beautiful country I have ever seen, we came to a cross-roads where we picked up a gillie—who I suppose was to act as a Staff Officer for the General's fishing—and then went on again up a long, winding road skirting a mountain.

Suddenly another typical Monty incident occurred. Although we were, as far as I could see, nowhere near any village, we came upon a stone building standing by the road, and above the hum of our engines I could hear the sound of children's voices singing. It was a village school. At once Monty ordered a halt. He got out, crossed the small playground in front of the building and went in through the open door.

The singing stopped abruptly. Then we heard frantic cheering, which presently died away. A precise voice began to speak. I couldn't hear what Monty said, but I imagine it was the sort of homely talk which you sometimes hear on speech days at school. By this time in his career Monty had grown to love young people. Later on he installed himself at the school in Surrey where he had sent his son. He loved to be with the boys. He would sit with them at meals, joke with them and set them puzzles.

It was certainly a strange situation, this line of cars drawn up by a remote school in the Highlands, with officers and men sitting in silence while their General gave an impromptu address to a classroom of bairns. All the more so as the world imagined him working day and night in preparation for the greatest invasion in history. He had that power of detaching himself completely from his worries and enjoying the passing moment.

Now the singing began again. "O God, our help in ages past," the piping voices sang. Monty came out looking happy, crossed the playground and got back into his car while teachers and children streamed out after him to cheer him on his way.

On the spur of a steep mountain which towered into the clouds we halted again.

" 'Ere we are, Sarge," said Taffy. "All change for the Elephant and Castle."

I got out and sidled up as near as I could to Monty. Everything was much more informal than it had been during the D-Day rehearsal. He was on holiday and he evidently meant to enjoy himself. There was a twinkle in his eye, and he reminded me of a friendly house-master on a day's outing with two or three schoolboys left in his charge after the end of term.

"Now, you chaps," he said briskly to the younger ones, "I think it would be a good plan if you made your way over the top of that hill. We will meet you on the other side. Don't be long—it's getting on for lunch-time."

The Captain and the other aides looked at the 'hill' which was a majestic mountain and tried to contort their faces into expressions of pleasurable anticipation.

I have noticed that when a party of people is gathered together for an outing there is often a comedian among them who keeps up a humorous running commentary. There was one among us now, a driver named Alf with a Cockney wit and a gift for imitating the General and his Staff *sotto voce*.

I heard Alf's voice behind me: "Wot price the Army marchin' on its stummick. This lot'll 'ave to 'ave a belly copter."

Taffy blew his nose violently. Imitating Monty's voice Alf went on: "Naow you fellers, pull your bloomers up and over Monty Blonk at the double. You will report to me in ten minutes' time for an 'igh tea of tripe and onions. Over the top and the best of luck!"

Putting a good face on it the aides set off gallantly up the slope, while Monty and the Brigadier walked briskly along the road. To anyone passing we must have looked a strange procession. First, a small, dapper man with a roll-top sweater and a black beret marching beside a huge Scots Brigadier, and a long way behind them—in fact, nearly out of sight—a crawling string of vehicles headed by the General's Rolls.

Being so far behind, the drivers behaved like schoolboys when the master is out of the room. If for any reason the General stopped, the cars pulled up at once and the drivers got out and began fooling about. But the moment Monty moved on again there was a rush to get back into the cars and drive on.

At one of these halts a driver climbed up a tree and the others began pelting him with clods of earth and fir-cones. In the middle of all this Monty's chauffeur shouted a warning as Monty moved on again, whereupon the driver crashed down from branch to branch like a baboon, jumped a ditch and got into his jeep just in time to keep his distance. It seemed an extraordinary thing that although Monty was so far away he could still exert such a strong influence over his men. But perhaps these monkeylike antics were more in the nature of a game. Some wag called them 'Monty's Musical Chairs'.

After about an hour of this sort of thing we reached a mountain river where we were joined by the aides, who to my surprise looked as fresh and cheerful as if they had just strolled down Piccadilly instead of scaling a mountain.

Monty greeted them with, "Had a good walk, you two?"

"Yes, thank you, sir," one of them replied.

"Did you get a good view from the top?"

"Wonderful, sir," said the Captain.

I heard Alf mutter, "Wunnerful view of the bottom of a double Scotch, if you arst me."

We moved on again until we came to a shooting lodge,

where the hampers were unpacked and Monty with his Staff sat in a circle on the grass. We drivers made ourselves comfortable against a wall some little distance off, but not too far for me to continue watching the General.

By this time I had recorded in my memory quite a number of things about him: his characteristic walk with his hands clasped behind his back, the way he pinched a little roll of flesh on his cheek when he was thinking, his sudden movements, his habit of throwing out one hand as he hammered home his points. But now came the question, how did he eat?

It may sound a small point, but I knew that before long I should be called upon to eat and drink in the Monty manner —for all I knew, under the close scrutiny of men who had eaten with him. A man can be watched intently when he is eating. If I made a slip it might be fatal. And so now I watched exactly how fast or slowly he ate, whether he talked or gestured while he was eating, and all the rest of it.

After lunch Monty and his gillie went off to fish and I was told to go with Taffy and the Brigadier. Taffy told me under his breath that we were bound for the Brigadier's ancestral home. It turned out to be a lovely old Highland mansion with a great forest on one side of it and on the other a loch which came almost to the outside walls. His beautiful wife and children, two bonny little boys in kilts, came out to greet us. It was a charming scene made somewhat poignant by the fact that the Lord of the Manse might never see his family again.

When I returned to the hotel Jack was anxious to know if I felt that I could pass for the General, and when I told him that I was fairly confident about it except for his voice, he asked me to give an impromptu performance.

So with my hands clasped behind my back and my head held rigidly in the Monty manner, I walked up and down the room giving preposterous advice, issuing fantastic orders, and every now and again sacking a Colonel or a Brigadier. I explained that the Air Force would drop five million dummy parachute troops which would exhaust the whole of the enemy's supply of ammunition, while the real striking force would march across the bed of the Channel with weights tied to their feet. By the time they arrived, Rommel and his men would be in Berlin receiving decorations from the Führer for exterminating the dummy army, and so nobody would know that we had landed. We both laughed so much that I could hardly go on.

I suppose it is a sense of the ludicrous which has carried the British Army through its long history of trials and misfortunes. Certainly this was so in the early days of the First World War.

I remember the day in 1914 when having managed to enlist at the age of seventeen I was told to report to the Hotel Cecil, in the Strand, for further orders. Arriving there I found a motley assortment of men ranging from near-schoolboys to grizzled veterans, and from taxi-drivers to City magnates. With memories of Mr. Jenkinson fresh in my head I pictured a fierce Sergeant-major with waxed moustaches reeling off my daily list of military duties, but in response to my question the man next me, who wore a monocle and a suit from Savile Row, said: "It's the jolly old pay day. Biff along, old bean, and collect your seven bob." Seeing me hesitate he added, "If I were you I'd push in right away before the boodle runs out."

So I edged my way to the front and gave my name to the N.C.O. who sat at the pay table. As I walked away with my seven shillings I noticed that some of the men who had been in front of me were drawing a second pay packet at one of the other tables.

I heard a youth who looked like a barrow boy say to another: "I got three packets. Wot abaht you?"

"Four," said the other. "Wot siy we 'op it and join up agin somewhere else?"

A tall, bored-looking officer called for silence.

"Now look here, you fellers, you're in the Army now. It's

a jolly good show, but we're short of N.C.O.s. If any of you know anything about drill, hand in your names for stripes. We'll parade in Hyde Park at 9 a.m. tomorrow."

His last words were greeted with a groan. "All right, then," he added, "let's say 9.30. Try not to be late, you chaps."

I glanced from this amiable officer to my unsoldierly-looking comrades-in-arms and thought perhaps the Army was not going to be so bad after all. Things seemed to have changed a bit since the Boer War. I think they changed still more between the two world wars.

The scene next morning in Hyde Park was unbelievable. Some of the men wore top-hats, morning coats and khaki trousers with puttees; others old Army tunics which apparently dated from the Boer War, with striped City trousers. Self-appointed N.C.O.s ran about trying to put us into some sort of order.

A ribald crowd gathered round us and began to cat-call and cheer our maiden efforts and even to shout fanciful words of command which added to the confusion. One lively-looking old man who may have fought in the Zulu War when younger kept shouting, "On the right of you—Savages! On the left of you—Savages!" in ironic comment of the way we were facing in different directions.

"Lumme," exclaimed another man, "they won't 'ave no need to fight. When they seen this lot the Jerries'll die of larfin'."

Another spectator, a little man with a scrubby moustache, amused himself by shouting "Encore!" every time we tied ourselves in a knot. He did this once too often, for a big, solemn-looking recruit broke ranks, walked up to him and knocked him down. Some of the crowd took exception to this and set upon the recruit, whereupon several more of us broke ranks and went to his rescue.

A constable who was watching the proceedings thought

that matters had gone far enough and blew his whistle. More policemen came running up and our critic was arrested. "Encore!" we all yelled as he was taken away.

At this time the German propaganda machine was in full blast trying to prove that the military power of Great Britain was insignificant and contemptible. Yet these recruits who so perfectly fitted the nickname of 'Fred Karno's Army' were later to form part of Kitchener's famous First Army, the finest volunteer force ever raised. Hitler made the same mistake with his sneers about British decadence. His famous jibe about 'military idiots' was by this time beginning to recoil on his head after Monty's victories in the Western Desert.

The next few days I tailed Monty, except when I was forbidden to, watching his every movement and trying to catch his fleeting expressions; and I began to realize that he had himself under control in a way that I have never seen paralleled.

The whole nation was on tenterhooks about the coming invasion which might easily become a blood-bath, and even a shattering defeat. And one of the exceptions to this general nervousness was the man who had most cause to worry, the man who was in charge of it. From what I saw of him I would compare him to a ship with a deep keel which prevented it from being carried away by cross-currents.

"It is absolutely vital," he wrote later, "that a C.-in-C. should keep himself from becoming immersed in details. He must spend a great deal of time in quiet thought and reflection. He will refuse to sit up late at night conducting the affairs of his Army; he will be well advised to withdraw to his tent or caravan after dinner at night."

He had already withdrawn to his private room in the train on the evening when I set out for my promised interview. As I made my way there I wished that I had some of his iron self-control and detachment. Far from being detached, I was as nervous as if I had been granted a Royal Audience at Buckingham Palace. As I knocked on his door I imagined myself standing tongue-tied while the steel-blue eyes were fixed on me waiting for me to speak.

A quiet voice said, "Come in." I opened the door. The General was sitting at his desk writing his daily diary, which he never failed to do. He stood up with a smile.

As we stood facing each other it was rather like looking at myself in a mirror. The likeness struck me as uncanny, and I realized how relieved MI 5 must have been when they found me and how horrified they were when I had wanted to back out of it. On the stage it is something if you can resemble a man after using every artifice of make-up, but in this case there was no need for false eyebrows, padded cheeks, or anything of that kind. I was extraordinarily like the General, and as I afterwards discovered, the two of us were remarkably alike when we were boys.

I don't know if similar thoughts were passing through his own mind, but at once he made me feel perfectly at ease, just as he had done when he first began talking to the men of the Eighth Army on his arrival in the Western Desert.

When I told him that I had been born in Perth, Australia, the ice was well and truly broken, for his father had been Bishop of Tasmania and the family had lived in Hobart. He talked about his father—how he had travelled round his huge diocese on foot or by boat, sometimes going off for weeks at a time into the bush. I thought this curiously like Monty's own behaviour in the field, with his revolutionary idea that a Commander-in-Chief should be well up in front making personal contact with his men.

As he talked he stood up again so that I had a close view of him from every angle. I was also trying to record in my mind the rather high-pitched, incisive tone of his voice and the way he chose his words. He never used high-flown phrases; some people have even described his speech as dry and arid.

He questioned me about my service in the First World War and about what I had done in civilian life. To my surprise I found that like Colonel Lester he knew quite a lot about the Stage, and he was very much amused when I told him that years before I had worked one-night stands all through Scotland.

Suddenly I realized that it was time for me to go. The time had passed like lightning.

Monty said: "You have a great responsibility, you know. Do you feel confident?"

While I was hesitating he added quickly: "I'm sure everything will be all right. Don't worry about it." And in that moment not only did my qualms vanish but I saw how Monty had only to tell an army that it could do the impossible and it just went and did it.

We shook hands and I went out.

Walking back to my hotel I thought of that slight figure sitting in his bare, unfurnished room completely alone with his burdens and I wondered how I should feel if I were in his shoes.

It was common knowledge that he was no yes-man and that he'd had a considerable say in the invasion plans. Also that in initiating new methods of strategy he had trodden on the corns of the orthodox and had stirred up feelings of hostility by his ruthless opposition to inefficiency. His enemies could do nothing against him while the invasion was pending, but at the first sign of failure on his part they were waiting to set on him like wolves. It was a terrible responsibility for a man to shoulder, but hadn't he shouldered an even bigger one when he had been flown out to the Western Desert to take over an army standing on its last legs before a victorious Rommel?

Since the end of the war I have heard more unjust and irresponsible criticism of Montgomery than I have heard of any other man. Soldiers have called him a 'killer' because, they said, he left them too long in the line. Have they forgotten that half-way through the Battle of El Alamein he withdrew his armour for a 36-hour rest to the dismay of his superiors? Do they know what we in the first war had to go through when we fought to the point of complete exhaustion and still were not relieved?

Often I have heard him described as a showman, a conceited mob orator of a General who was for ever courting popularity among his men. All I can say is that if he was a showman he used his showmanship to brilliant effect and got extremely worthwhile results.

One of his post-war dictums was that the prime duty of a Commander-in-Chief in the field was to create an 'atmosphere', a kind of aura of courage and confidence in which his Staff and his subordinate commanders with their troops could live, work and fight.

This is what he set out to do the moment he first landed in Africa. The troops mistrusted Brass-hats; they had been let down once too often. And so he stuck a black beret on his head and talked to the Pit and Gallery in a way that no General in the field had ever talked before.

"Every single soldier must know, before he goes into battle, how the little battle he is fighting fits into the larger picture," he wrote. "The troops must be brought to a state of wild enthusiasm."

Before the very gates of Cairo he issued an order that there was to be no more retreating, and then going among his soldiers he convinced them that they were going to stand fast against Rommel's expected attack and a little later hit them for six. He even explained his plans to the Other Ranks. And they believed this strange little General whom nobody had heard of and who popped up in the desert from nowhere.

People said he was conceited and overbearing. This was not at all the impression which I got in my contacts with him. The hall-mark of conceit is a divorce from reality, a flight into a world of fantasy where a man sees things as they are not. But Monty was a thorough-going realist. In warfare he saw things as they really were, and before they happened he accurately predicted their course. Since he often knew better than most other people and was almost invariably proved right, they were slow to forgive him.

He had such a grasp of a military situation that it must have been galling for him when his superiors insisted on taking what in his view was the wrong course. No wonder that at times he seemed a little overbearing. Those who are dubious about something find it easy to be swayed this way and that, but a man who sees clearly what should be done must have a terrible feeling of exasperation when he cannot get others to agree with him. In all my dealings with him he always struck me as never in the least doubt about what he wanted to do, how it was to be done, and the complete rightness of his own point of view.

CHAPTER X

THE STRANGEST REHEARSAL
ON RECORD

RETURNING from this memorable interview I went into the bar of the hotel to see if I could find Jack, but he was not there. As I was having a drink an old man with a gnarled, unshaven face and bloodshot eyes tugged at my sleeve and motioned me aside. I was expecting him to try cadging a drink from me but instead of this he assumed a dark air of secrecy.

"Excuse me," he began, "but are you concairned wi' the General?"

"Why do you ask?" I replied guardedly.

He became even more mysterious. "It's none o' my business, likely, but there's queer things going on in yon woods. Ye see, I go oot o' nichts——"

"Poaching?"

"I'm no sayin' it's that, mon, but this is no poachin' matter. Ye see, I went oot the nicht"—he put his lips down to my ear—"and yon woods is full o' Gairmans! It's the General they're after, I'm thenken."

It was so fantastic that I couldn't help laughing, and at this moment Jack came into the bar.

"What's the joke?" he asked.

"No joke at all. This Security man here, thinly disguised as a Scottish laird, reports that the woods are full of Germans."

Jack uttered an expressive monosyllable.

"They've come here to kidnap the General."

Jack looked at the poacher, who solemnly nodded confirmation of my statement.

"And do you know who's going to save him?" I asked.

"Young Topping of the Naval Division, I suppose," said Jack and ordered a double Scotch.

"No, Lieutenant Jack Hervey, Popular Jack, with his little bow and arrow."

We soon forgot the incident, but next morning a middle-aged farmer buttonholed Jack outside the hotel and told him that he and others of the local inhabitants were rather worried about something. The woods beyond the railway were full of soldiers who seemed to be talking German.

Jack began to suspect that his leg was being pulled. "Who started this yarn?" he asked. "No enemy troops could land here without being seen."

But the farmer refused to be put off. He repeated that the woods were full of Germans who appeared to be tough paratroopers, and he thought that General Montgomery was in grave danger.

Jack told me all this later in the day, and absurd as the news seemed to be, neither of us could forget it. We kept returning to it and at last almost convinced ourselves that it was just possible that some parachute troops had been dropped by night in this lonely part of Scotland and were lying in wait to make a sortie and assassinate Monty. I pointed out that it was Jack's duty to deal with this desperate move on the enemy's part, and I drew a glowing picture of his last stand on a mountain of enemy dead, waving a Union Jack and brandishing a sword.

Jack retaliated by offering to reconnoitre and insisting that I go with him. As I couldn't see how to get out of it we set off together in the dark that night. Except for the hooting of an owl, all was quiet, We reached the edge of the woods and stood still, straining our ears.

Presently to my horror we heard the unmistakable sound of gruff voices and faint lights showed through the trees.

"Wait here," said Jack, and disappeared into the gloom.

Five minutes later he was back again. "Paratroops," he said shortly. "I was never nearer death in my life."

"Good God!"

"Polish," he added. "A sentry covered me with his rifle and my past life came up again. I don't know a word of Polish, or why he didn't pull the trigger."

When we got back to the hotel we found our friend the poacher waiting for us in the bar. We explained to him that the paratroops were not Germans but Poles.

He shook his head. "Nae, nae, they'll be Hitler's men," he said decisively. "They wouldna let me tak a rabbit."

When my stay in Scotland had come to an end and I told Colonel Lester about this he hardly listened. He was much more interested to hear whether anyone had had any doubts about my being a *bona-fide* I.C. Sergeant. In fact, on reporting to him at the War Office he put me through quite a gruelling cross-examination.

After I had answered his questions he again said, "The General is very pleased with the way you have done your job so far."

How on earth did he know? I wondered. I would have taken my oath that he hadn't been on the phone to Monty. Security reasons alone made it very unlikely. Had he been in Dalwhinnie under my very nose disguised as a Scots ghillie?

He went on to warn me for the fiftieth time against opening my mouth too wide. I admit that I was beginning to get rather tired of these never-ending cautions and I even thought that MI5 were unnecessarily fussy. But after the war was over I heard a story which made me think again. The truth is that even the most reticent people are occasionally subject to indiscreet moods.

Some time after D-Day it was discovered that there had been a grave leakage of information about our secret plans, and an officer of MI5 was sent to France to find out how the leak had occurred. He spent days cautiously questioning scores of people, hoping for a chance word which might put him on the track of the culprit, but he drew a complete blank. He was about to return to England and report his failure when a casual word or two from a Staff Officer sent him to one of the Top Brass in the R.A.F. who blandly admitted to being the guilty party!

Where I was concerned, MI 5 forgot nothing, and looking back on it now, I am convinced that they never did an unnecessary thing or spoke one word too many. Although I was told that I should have to fly, I had no idea where I should fly to.

As far as anyone knew, Monty had never been air-sick in his life. Very well, I must be given some air training. One morning the Colonel asked me to go to the Devonshire Club, St. James's Street, where I met a young, good-looking Wing Commander of the Canadian Air Force. In Kensington we picked up an R.A.F. officer who was a friend of the Wing Commander and drove to Northolt aerodrome.

It was a lovely day, and not knowing what was in store for me I enjoyed the run down. But on arrival there the Wing Commander said casually, "I've had orders to take you up to see if you're O.K. for flying," and both of them disappeared into the control building.

In this modern age of air travel it may seem absurd that I was petrified by this news, but the fact was I had never flown before and heights always made me feel ill.

Presently they came out of the building and I followed them across the aerodrome. We came to a huge plane with seats for about thirty passengers. Oh good, I thought, this isn't so bad. I can at least hide in the back and they won't notice when I'm being ill. But they walked past it.

Behind it was something which looked like an old Austin Seven with two wings and a tail stuck on to it. The Wing Commander went up to it, lifted up a sort of cover and said, "Jump in, James."

I clambered up and wriggled myself into a tiny bucket-seat in the back. They too got in and sat in front of me. "You'd better put your safety belt on," said the Wing Commander, turning round. "Oh no, I forgot, you can't bail out of this type of aircraft." He shouted something, pulled the cover over us and the engine started up.

The plane rocked and swayed about. Not daring to look over the side, I took out an envelope and pencil and with my eyes glued to the paper I slowly wrote some lines from a burlesque on a play called *Three Weeks* in which I had appeared years ago.

> Three weeks to get a son and heir!
> How in the Elinor Glynne am I going to do it?
> Black sheets, shaded lights, and—
> You and I, darling.

We were off the ground. Cautiously I peeped round. Nothing but blue sky with a few fleecy clouds. I held my breath and looked down—and I felt fine; the sense of height didn't affect me at all.

In half an hour we were over Salisbury Plain, and soon after that we made a perfect landing at an R.A.F. station in Devon. I never felt better in my life.

After the flight I was driven back to London by a Wing Commander who turned out to be Dennis Wheatley, the well-known author. En route we ran short of petrol and we drew up at a camp for American coloured troops for a fill-up. A big buck negro at the gates gave us an expansive grin instead of a salute and waved us on. When we pulled up by the petrol pump another negro thrust his head in at the window and greeted the officer beside me with a "Hiya, boss."

Our driver got out and took him by the arm. "Any chance of some petrol, mate?"

"Petrawl? Noa, we ain't nuth'n like that, I reckon. If it's

gas you'se wantin', jes turn de handle, Limey, and out she comes."

The driver began to get annoyed. "My moniker ain't Limey, old cock."

"How come, big boy? I sure never heard of Limey Alcock."

"For God's sake! What about this petrol? Have you got a requisition form for me to fill in?"

The darkie scratched his woolly head. "Rekwizon form? No, suh, I ain't never heard of that thing." He grinned broadly. "There's the gas, borss. Jes turn de handle and out she comes."

So we gave it up and turned the handle.

Next morning Colonel Lester told me that the time was getting very near for the curtain to go up. Was I certain that I was ready? I replied that I had studied Monty under a variety of conditions and had watched him in his different moods. I felt confident that I was ready and that if I studied him any more I might get stale.

My General's uniform had already been made and there was now a discussion about Monty's numerous medal ribbons and the exact order in which they should be worn. Eventually his tailor was consulted about it, after which I set out with Stephen Watts and Jack Hervey to buy my kit for the Near East. This was my first definite clue as to where I was going.

As we walked down Piccadilly I remembered something.

"You know I shall need a gold watch-chain, don't you?"

They stared at me. "A gold watch-chain," said Jack. "Haven't you got a wrist-watch?"

"What grade of Intelligence Officers are you two? M.D.? Don't you know that Monty always wears a gold watch-chain across his battle-dress?"

"All right, all right, you shall have it," Stephen said. "No expense shall be spared to dress you for the part." And he went into Woolworth's and bought a handsome gold chain for half a crown. Although I have no financial interest in Woolworth's,

H

I will say it was remarkably good value. All the time I was General Montgomery I wore it with a key on one end of it and a penknife on the other. Luckily no one asked me for the time.

When we had made our purchases I spent the rest of the day watching Monty on the news-reels, probably for the last time. Next morning I was to report for my first rehearsal. I couldn't imagine what it would be like. I have been to some strange rehearsals in my time but evidently this would be the strangest of them all.

One of these rehearsals came into my mind next morning on my way to the War Office. Years ago I was to appear in a play at Seaham Harbour, Durham. The Manager of the local theatre had lost the theatre key and so we had to rehearse in a field outside it where cows were grazing.

The first mishap occurred when the leading man who had to kneel before the heroine chose an unfortunate place on the grass to do it. You can imagine the state of his trouser knees, but I doubt if you can imagine his language. He was in such a bad temper that he started to have a row with his brother who was putting the show on. The quarrel flared up so fiercely that they came to blows, and his brother landed him one on the nose.

Few actors can resist the temptation to act off the stage. Holding his handkerchief to his bleeding nose, the leading man turned the situation into High Drama.

"This is too much," he exclaimed oratorically. "I quit. Find another to take my part—if you can."

He stalked across to the ancient Ford in which he had arrived, took hold of the starting handle, then straightened up and shouted: "I wash my hands of your piffling production. I will not sully my name by appearing in such trash. Good-bye!"

He bent down and jerked the starting handle several times, but the engine refused to start.

Straightening his back again he waved his arm and cried, "And so, I bid you farewell!"

Once again he worked at the starter but still the engine refused to fire. At last, releasing the brake, he yelled, "To hell with you all!" and amid a roar of laughter he pushed his car down the road. It was the perfect anticlimax.

As soon as I entered the well-known room at the War Office I felt an atmosphere of tension. The Colonel was there with Jack and Stephen and a tall, grey-haired man who was introduced to me as Brigadier Heywood. This last man was to act as my personal aide during the impersonation. There was also a young Captain, Moore by name, who was to take charge of our hold-alls.

I liked the Brigadier from the first. He had been with MI 5 for many years, and no doubt had been very carefully chosen for what might prove to be an extremely ticklish job. He looked to me like a man whom nothing could rattle, and like Monty he radiated a feeling of strength and confidence.

Colonel Lester wasted no time. "Now, James," he began, "I will give you a brief outline of the first part of our plans. Tomorrow evening at 6.30 you will be taken to an address in London where you will change your uniform—and become General Montgomery. You will be driven to the airport, giving the public a chance to see you en route. We want just a little advance publicity, and we hope that one or two nameless individuals whom we have under observation will get to know about your movements.

"On reaching the airport you will find certain high-ranking officers of the Army and Air Force parading on the airfield to see you off. Also the skipper and crew of the Prime Minister's private plane in which you will travel. It will be something of a ceremonial occasion. As you get out of your car you salute, inspect the parade of officers; then go over to the skipper, say a word or two to him and board the plane. Is this clear?"

"Yes, sir."

"I can give you only the general directions. You must manage the details in your own way—just as you think Monty would do it."

"Yes, sir."

"Right. Now, gentlemen, we'll take the first scene."

The room, perhaps not for the first time in its history, became a small theatre. Chairs and tables were placed to represent the plane, the crew and the parade of officers.

As we took our places I saw that I had been right. This was certainly the most fantastic rehearsal that I had ever attended.

"I and these chairs here are the high-ranking officers," said Colonel Lester. "You, Stephen, are the skipper and you, Jack, the crew of the plane. This chair is the car."

The Brigadier put his arm round my waist and solemnly we shuffled along to the chair, representing the car's arrival. Then I turned, and as General Montgomery I stepped out of the car, saluted, went over to the line of officers on my left, gravely walked along the row of chairs; then over to the skipper and his crew, returned the skipper's salute, and in Monty's precise tones I remarked, "Hope we have a good trip."

Stephen replied smoothly: "Yes, sir, I hope so. The weather reports are excellent."

After this I turned, marked time to show that I was walking up the gangway, turned again to give a farewell salute and sat down in one of the chairs representing the plane.

"Good," said Colonel Lester. "I can't see much wrong with that."

We went through it once or twice more and then we sat down and he offered me a cigarette.

"You won't be able to have many more of these," he said, holding the lighter. "Better start cutting them down after this. As soon as you're Monty you'll be a strict non-smoker."

While I was smoking it he told me a little more. "You're now in the air. Monty has left England in full view of scores of

people. If any of them happen to be enemy agents, so much
the better. You fly through the night to Gibraltar, where you
will be landing at 7.45 a.m., to be received by the Governor.

"When somebody important arrives at a British colony or
station which has a Governor, the rule is that the Governor
never comes out in person to meet his guest, but he sends a
representative to act for him. When you land at the airport you
will find a full parade of senior officers waiting to receive you.
Salute them, then turn and ask for Major Foley, who by the
way is in the know. Talk to him for a few moments in the
Monty manner, then get into the Governor's car which will
take you in state through the streets of Gib. to Government
House."

He waited a few moments to enable me to digest all this.
"You have probably heard some criticism of us—how we are
always being caught on the wrong foot, always too late, and
so on? As a matter of fact we rather welcome this sort of thing
—it's a good thing to get the enemy to underestimate you—but
I need hardly tell you, this picture of us is not quite accurate.
Sometimes we deliberately give the impression that we are
committing terrible bloomers. This is what we are going to do
in Gibraltar.

"When you get there you'll find the usual crowd of curious
onlookers watching the plane arrive, and among them some
Spanish workers who have jobs at the airport. Several of them
will be enemy agents. We have already spread the rumour that
General Montgomery is arriving in the Near East on a very
secret visit and that he wants it kept strictly quiet. Our people
have made certain that this news has reached the ears of enemy
agents. So you see why you've got to be perfect in your part.
Every move of yours will be watched intently by clever people
who are working for Hitler."

"Spanish workmen?"

"Yes, and not only Spaniards. Gib. is a hot-bed of es-
pionage. Now to get back to your arrival there. Your car

pulls up at Government House, the guard presents arms, the main doors open, and out steps your old friend General Sir Ralph Eastwood, Governor of Gibraltar, to welcome you."

"My old friend, sir?"

"Yes. You and Sir Ralph were at Sandhurst together and you greet each other with some warmth. 'Hullo, Monty,' the Governor will say, and you will reply, 'Well, Rusty, it's good to see you again,' or words to that effect. Then he'll take your arm and lead you inside, with your aides following you. After that, it's up to you. Play it off your cuff."

"Is the Governor in the know?"

"Yes, of course. But don't forget, inside Government House you will be under close observation from people who mustn't know. There's the steward, for instance, who was once Monty's batman and has known him intimately for years. From what I have seen of you I believe you've mastered the role pretty thoroughly and you could probably fool most of the enemy agents you're likely to meet, but this man knows every hair of Monty's head and he'll be waiting on you at table, I expect. Do you think you can fool *him*?"

"I don't know, sir, I'll try."

"It's the acid test. If *he* takes you for Monty you needn't be afraid anyone else will see through you."

One of the things which struck me in my dealings with MI5 was their rule of telling me only just enough to take me over the next lap. Having run this lap, more information would be given me at the next relay starting-point, perhaps by some person thousands of miles away. It was rather like a treasure hunt with clues at widely separated points.

I was not surprised when Colonel Lester said: "Sir Ralph will give you further instructions which I won't burden you with now. What I want you to do is to concentrate on what you're doing at the moment and not try to think too far ahead. Remember, we can plan and time things this end; we can train you and tell you more or less what to do; but things never work out exactly as they are planned. The scheme has got to be flexible, and this is where your own initiative comes in.

"Once you are launched on this adventure you must paddle your own canoe. I know on the stage mistakes can be made and other members of the cast can cover them up. But you can't expect any leniency on the World Stage. A single slip may ruin one of the greatest plans of deception that has ever been attempted."

In our previous conversations he had always been careful not to say anything which might make me nervous, but now he had spoken very gravely, and from his expression I sensed a doubt in his mind that he had been a little too alarmist.

"I feel pretty sure of myself now, sir," I said. "Whatever happens I won't let you down."

"I am certain you won't," he replied, giving me a very straight look. "But it's not *me* you have to think of, it's the thousands of men whose lives depend on you."

After this little interlude we rehearsed the landing at Gibraltar with chairs to represent the car, the plane, the Top Brass and Major Foley. Disembarking from my plane and followed by my two aides, one of whom carried a book of the King's Regulations to represent my hold-all, I saluted the row of officers, then said, "Good morning, gentlemen, where is Foley?"

When you come to think of it, it is only natural that MI 5 men should be good mimics. Mimicry is a form of humour which can relieve a tense situation, and also it can come in very handy if you happen to be concealing your identity.

Before Jack could answer, the Colonel replied, "Yus, 'ere I am, old cock," which had us all in fits of laughter.

We went through the scene again and everything went well except that I turned too quickly and collided with the Brigadier.

"I'm sorry, sir," I exclaimed, but immediately he dug me in the ribs and said, "Don't call me sir—I have to call *you* sir."

Colonel Lester, who had noticed the incident, gave me a short curtain lecture. From now on, he said, I must try to get the feeling of actually being General Montgomery. I must change my inner attitude towards the world. Self-confidence must replace timidity. I must carry an imaginary picture of myself as a successful General. Senior officers must be senior officers no longer but mere subordinates. If crowds cheered me it would only be my due. If I inspected parades I must never stop to consider if *I* were coming up to scratch but only whether *they* were. This feeling of actually *being* Monty must govern everything and show itself in my behaviour.

Stephen Watts, who of course knows a lot about the Theatre, did much to help us with these rehearsals. We had to get every movement and gesture accurate, and the timing as meticulous as it is in a West End play.

We rehearsed the next scene, my arrival at Government House. Jack was Sir Ralph Eastwood and Colonel Lester the Guard of Honour. I alighted from my imaginary car and was about to return the Guard's salute when I was almost overcome by the absurdity of the situation. The Colonel stood there as stiff as a ramrod, his battered hat perched on his head and his umbrella held smartly at the Present!

Mounting the steps of Government House I was met by a smiling Jack who exclaimed, "Hullo, Monty, how are you?"

"Hullo, Rusty," I replied heartily, shaking him by the hand, "it's good to see you again." And together we turned and entered the building.

We went through this scene once or twice until Stephen was satisfied; but suddenly his expression changed.

"Good Lord!" he said. "Your right hand!"

All eyes were turned on my hand which had been badly

damaged in the First World War. The middle finger was missing, and within twenty-four hours I was to be General Montgomery who seldom wore gloves.

Time and again I was to discover the ingenuity and resourcefulness of MI 5. Perhaps it was not surprising that no one had noticed it before. When I was first faced with this disability I trained myself to conceal it. I had to do this as an actor. On the stage I always worked with my right hand behind me or in my pocket, and in course of time it became second nature to do this off-stage as well. Some friends did not spot it for months, and in fact one friend told me it was a whole year before he noticed it. After a moment's silence Colonel Lester sent Jack out to make some purchases in a chemist's shop, and when he returned they made a most realistic middle finger out of cotton wool, adhesive plaster and some stiffening material. Strapped on to my hand and coloured to match my skin, it would have needed a very sharp pair of eyes to detect it.

I began to wonder whether we had overlooked anything else.

"By the way," I said, "you spoke about an ex-batman of the General's who knows his habits exactly. What does Monty eat?"

Nobody spoke. "What I mean is," I went on, "he may be a vegetarian or a food faddist, and it would never do to break his rules."

"H'm," said Colonel Lester. "What does he eat? Do any of you know?" They all shook their heads.

"Very well, I'll have to see him at once and ask him."

That same evening, he went down to the South Coast and had a strange conversation with the General which went something like this.

Col. Lester: I'm sorry to trouble you, sir, but what do you eat?

Monty: What do you mean, what do I eat?

Col. Lester: When James impersonates you he'll have to eat just what you do. Are there any peculiarities in your diet?

Monty: Certainly not. I don't eat meat, I don't eat fish, and I take no milk or sugar with my porridge. That's all.

CHAPTER XI

A FEARFUL DILEMMA

I HEARD all this next morning when we had our final rehearsals. The time for action was getting very near now and
when Jack and Stephen took me out for lunch I noticed that
they shepherded me across the road crossings as if I were
Royalty. With only a few hours to go it would have been
disastrous to let me get run over. In the bar of the Berkeley
Hotel they did their best to keep me cheerful, which was not
so easy considering that I had to drink ginger ale without
even a cigarette to console me.

Peter Cheyney came in and I wondered what he would
have thought had he known what 'copy' was standing there
within a few feet of him.

Appearances are often very deceptive. During lunch I
remember noticing a slovenly-looking officer who was droop-
ing over the back of a chair talking to a girl.

"What a wet-looking bloke," I said. "I wonder how he
got a commission."

Stephen replied: "He's just come back after his fifth
parachute drop in Northern Italy. He speaks six languages
and works with the Resistance Movement. He's one of the
bravest chaps I know."

Since then I have made it a rule never to criticize anyone
in uniform. You just can't tell unless you happen to know a
man intimately.

Our rehearsal room was crowded when we returned to it
after lunch. Besides the Secret Service people and my two
aides, I found two Army officers and a civilian. A screen had
been put up at the end of the room and beside it stood a camera
on a stand.

"This is our last rehearsal," Colonel Lester said. "It's the Dress Rehearsal. Behind the screen you'll find your uniform, and when you're ready we're going to have some photos taken. Mr. Churchill wants to see them."

I went behind the screen and saw a table, a chair, a tall mirror, and hanging over the back of another chair a full General's battle-dress with a black beret and a fleece-lined leather jacket.

As I sat down and studied my face in the mirror, a scared creature who looked about as much like a successful General as a hypnotized rabbit stared back at me, and I was overcome by the worst fit of stage-fright I had had yet.

I don't know how long I sat there before professional pride began to come to my rescue. I studied my face again and saw that I needed hardly any make-up at all. Just a touch of grease-paint to grey my temples. I trimmed my moustache almost to vanishing point, brushed up my eyebrows to make them bristle, then put on the uniform with its five rows of ribbons and the gold chain from pocket to pocket.

There is an old saying in the Theatre: "Once you get your make-up on, it will all come to you." Adjusting the black beret with its badge of the Armoured Corps, I looked at my reflection again and all my self-confidence came back with a rush. With my hands clasped behind my back, I drew a deep breath and came out from behind the screen.

I don't suppose any actor has had a more nerve-racking audition. Eight pairs of eyes studied me in dead silence; then there was a sort of gasp as each man turned away to hide his feelings. I knew that I had made a hit.

Colonel Lester, whose face expressed intense relief, posed me for several photographs, and after the photographer had gone he began to give me my final instructions.

"When you leave Government House you will be driven to the airport, sitting beside the Governor. On arrival there you will find all the Top Brass drawn up to see you off. This is much the same pattern as before, but now there is something additional."

He gave me a wintry smile. "You may remember that I have warned you once or twice about the necessity of keeping your mouth shut. Well, at this point you have got to forget this and open it as wide as you like. You've got to give the impression of having swallowed a dose of the Truth Drug, though what you say must of course be the purest invention. There's a good reason for this. By now every enemy agent in Gib. will have heard of your visit and will be there to see you leave.

"So get out of your car and throw your weight about as if you were giving last instructions in secret. Don't be afraid to let yourself go. Take Sir Ralph by the arm and draw him apart. Be madly indiscreet, but try to make it plausible. Mention the War Cabinet and Secret Plans. Talk to him earnestly as if you were so intent on impressing last-minute instructions on his mind that you were oblivious of the danger of being overheard.

"And don't forget to give everyone a good look at you. Walk up and down with him as if absorbed in vital conversation. Change your manner occasionally. Point to certain parts of the harbour as if you had noticed changes since your last visit to the Rock. Remind him of past incidents. Do you see what I mean?"

"Yes, sir."

"Right. After you have taken off from Gibraltar the Brigadier will give you your instructions for the next scene. Gib. isn't the only place you're bound for. You'll be travelling all through the Middle East."

We rehearsed my departure from Gib. and then I changed back into my own uniform.

Colonel Lester seemed satisfied. "We've got over most of our hurdles for the time being," he said. "All I want you to do now is to relax. Take it easy for a bit. Don't worry. Enjoy yourself."

I thought of the teetotal, smokeless evening which lay before me, with the heavy feeling of Zero Hour hanging over me like a thunder-cloud, and I wondered if this was a piece of sarcasm. Jack and Stephen, who knew quite well how I felt, took me out to tea at the Piccadilly Hotel. I must say they worked as hard to keep me cheerful as a couple of comedians at a Command Performance. I thought of the sacrificial victim among the Aztecs who was fêted for a whole month before being offered up on the altar. How I wished that I possessed some of Monty's phlegm—Monty who after an intense day's fighting in the Western Desert when the issue hung perilously in the balance would retire for the night and simply order himself to sleep.

The evening wore on and we finished up at the Café Royal in Regent Street. By this time I had lost my appetite and the whole thing had become like an uneasy dream.

At 6.45, with only half an hour to go, we took a taxi to the Brigadier's flat in Kensington where I found Colonel Lester and my two aides waiting for me. This time the Colonel acted as my dresser. The Brigadier's wife, a charming woman, brought me coffee and sandwiches. When I apologized for turning the bedroom into a dressing-room, she told me that so many strange things occurred in the flat that she never gave them a second thought.

When I had donned my General's uniform we sat down together for our last conversation.

"I'm not going to give you a pep talk," he said with a grin. "Provided you don't worry you'll be absolutely all right. You won't be alone. The Brigadier will always be there to help you. But if you're 'on the stage' and get stuck, just play it off your cuff.

"Now about money. You know, don't you, that this job is simply part of your duties as a soldier? It was suggested to the War Cabinet that you should be paid danger money——"

"Danger money, sir?"

"Oh yes, you'll be in danger all right. But the Treasury said no, you couldn't draw extra pay for carrying out your duties. However, General Montgomery got to hear this and he took a strong line about it. He said, 'If James is good enough to wear my uniform he's good enough to draw my pay.' "

I thought of the austere, kindly man I had met in Dalwhinnie, sitting alone in his bare room, and I was surprised to find my eyes filling with tears.

"That's very good of him," was all I could say.

"By the way," said Colonel Lester, "what pay does he get?"

"What pay does he get, sir?"

"Dammit, you ought to know. You're in the Pay Corps, aren't you?"

"Yes, sir, but I've never had to deal with a General's account."

I suppose that at this critical hour just before the curtain rose Colonel Lester for all his apparent sang-froid was feeling a little on edge. I know I was. He thought me an idiot for not knowing a General's pay, and I thought him unreasonable for expecting me to know it. We almost glared at each other. Then both of us saw the absurdity of getting heated over such a trifling matter at a moment like this.

"Oh well, we won't worry about that now," he said. "There's one last thing. Here are a dozen khaki handkerchiefs each marked with the General's initials, B.L.M. In the course of your travels I want you to drop these about as if by accident wherever you think fit. You see the idea? If anyone has any suspicions that you're not Monty, discovering one of these should give him a little reassurance. The written word abideth. In this game it's the little details that count."

He had said, "There's one last thing," which meant that his

job was done and that it was time for us to say good-bye. I
looked at this strange man of many parts and thought of all
that had happened since first I met him at the Grand Hotel.
In a short time we had come a long way together, and now
that I was to lose him I felt as if I were losing a lifelong
friend.

"I'll say good-bye now," he said, "because I may not have
another chance. When once the curtain goes up you mustn't
even *think* of yourself as James. All the best of luck to you."

He gripped my hand hard and went out of the room, leaving
a terrible feeling of loneliness behind him.

Quickly I set my beret at the correct angle, turned my
wrist-watch inwards, adjusted the false finger and practised one
or two salutes to make certain it was firmly secured, picked up
the small Bible like the one Monty always carried and put it in
my hold-all, and I was ready for the opening scene.

Stephen, Jack and my two aides were waiting for me in the
next room, and all four of them stared at me critically just as
they had done before. And again I felt a lessening of the tension and a general sense of relief.

The first two shook me by the hand with a "Cheero,
Jimmy, see you when you come back. All the best." The
Brigadier said heartily: "I'm certain you'll be a big success. I'll
see you at the airport, sir."

"Thanks, Heywood," I replied, giving him one of Monty's
quick smiles. I led the way down, followed by the Brigadier
and Captain Moore, my second aide, carrying my hold-all. At
the front door I paused for a moment. Outside were three
Army cars, and a crowd had gathered round the leading one
which flew Monty's pennant. This at last was my entrance
on to the stage which I had imagined so many times in the last
few weeks.

As I made my way to the leading car the crowd stared at
me in deep curiosity. Returning the driver's salute, I got in and

FIELD-MARSHAL VISCOUNT MONTGOMERY OF ALAMEIN, G.C.B., D.S.O.

THE GOVERNOR'S PALACE AT GIB-RALTAR First stage in the Great Adventure Here Clifton James, posing as "Monty", hoodwinked two of Hitler's top agents

Photo Keystone

Courtesy Imperial War Museum

LIEUTENANT-GENERAL SIR RALPH EASTWOOD, K.C.B., D.S.O., M.C. Sir Ralph was at Sandhurst with Field-Marshal Montgomery As Governor and Commander-in-Chief, Gibraltar, he was host to "Monty's Double" and played a highly successful role in the Great Deception sat down in the left-hand seat at the back. I was feeling a little dazed.

A cheer went up from the crowd, and then the door on my right opened and Colonel Lester jumped in.

"They're cheering you," he hissed in my ear. "Salute, wave to them. You're Monty!"

Next moment he was gone. As my car moved off, the crowd cheered again and I heard shouts of "Good old Monty!" In my anxiety to play my part I had clean forgotten to play to the audience. Looking out of the window I gave them a brilliant Monty smile and the famous Monty salute. As we sped down Kensington High Street people came running towards us from all directions.

It was the same when we stopped at the traffic lights. The pennant drew people as if by magic. They cheered and waved, and I smiled and saluted them in return until the muscles of my face were stiff and my arm began to ache.

MI 5 must have discreetly advertised the news that Monty was leaving for Northolt aerodrome because when we got there a crowd of civilians stood by the gates. Rows of Air Force personnel lined the approaches while a detachment of military policemen on motor-cycles escorted us front and rear.

As we came to a halt on the airfield the scene was just as I had pictured it. Drawn up in front of my plane was a row of smart R.A.F. men with a young Wing Commander in front of them. On the left I saw a formidable array of high-ranking officers of the Army and Navy.

My heart was pounding like a piston and for a moment I thought I should be unable to get out of the car and go through with it. Then something inside me gave way. The fear and the paralysis were coming from Lieutenant James. With a violent effort I pushed James aside and became Monty. From that moment the James side of me receded more and more into the background as the hours passed, until it became hardly more than a memory. If I had not been able to perform this psychological trick I should never have been able to do what I did.

Stepping briskly out of the car and smiling a little, I heard the senior officer call his top-rank party to attention. He saluted and I returned his salute. Followed by the Brigadier, I slowly walked along the ranks of these veterans and then went over to the crew of the aircraft.

I was now about to speak my first lines, and I offered up a silent prayer thay they would be absolutely convincing.

"How are you, Slee?" I asked. "D'you think we shall have a good trip?"

"I think so, sir," he replied, standing stiffly to attention. "The weather reports are quite favourable."

"Good, good," I said. After slowly inspecting the air crew I went up the gangway, turned to give everyone a last salute and then entered the plane.

Most actors know that sense of relief which comes to them when they have successfully weathered their first scene. My own relief was heightened by the lavish appointments of the aircraft—the beautiful padded seats which tilted back, the perfectly equipped miniature kitchen and the bathroom.

The engines roared and presently we were airborne, climbing steadily and headed for Spain. I thought of what had happened in the last five minutes. All those high-ranking officers, some of whom knew Monty intimately, who had really believed they were honouring *him* when they were turning out in all their glory for Lieutenant James of the Pay Corps. And suddenly I remembered old Dr. Hicks banging on the front door and then rapidly shuffling round to the back in his disgraceful trousers, chuckling, "Tricked them again!" and I burst out laughing.

Feeling a hand on my shoulder I turned round and saw the Brigadier looking at me with concern written all over his face. I'm certain he thought I was hysterical, but in the roar of the engines I could hardly explain to him what the joke was.

However, by getting our heads close together we managed to have a short conversation.

"How are you feeling?" he asked.

"Not too bad, thanks." I took off my beret and stretched my legs.

"I'll bet you're feeling pretty bad. But if it's any consolation to you, you were simply splendid. Dying for a smoke, are you?"

"Nearly dead. But what's the use?"

"You're off duty for another seven hours. I should think we might risk it if you're careful."

He gave me a cigarette, and when I had lit it he handed me the top of a thermos flask.

"It's all right," I said, "I'm not feeling sick."

He laughed. "I know that. It's to catch the ash. When we get to Gib. someone might spot the ash and begin to suspect that you're not Monty."

"It might be your ash."

"What, with Monty in front of me? Unlikely."

I remembered how in my early youth I had smoked tea leaves and shavings in an old pipe of the Doctor's and what a fuss there had been when Aunt Kitty had caught me in the act. Monty had also been caught smoking when he was a boy, and his father, the Bishop, had taken him into the chapel and the two of them had prayed about it. It was very characteristic of him that he would never give his promise not to smoke or drink, but that when he was old enough to do as he liked he had become a non-smoker and a teetotaller.

Time passed. The skipper of the aircraft came along and the three of us sat talking under a brilliant moon which lit up a lovely carpet of fleecy clouds stretching into the far distance.

Two incidents concerned with my departure from England and my voyage to Gibraltar stick in my memory, though I did not know about them at the time they happened.

After my plane had left Northolt there was some conversation among the high-ranking officers, and none of them had any suspicions about the identity of the man they had just seen off. One of them, who had been on Monty's Staff, remarked that the old man looked very fit but a bit tired.

The other incident the Brigadier told me about while we flew above the moonlit clouds. Standing some twenty yards from the parade of high-ups he had spotted a civilian in a dark suit and a battered hat. As he was going up the gangway into the plane he looked back and saw that the figure was standing close to him. Colonel Lester had winked and made a rude gesture as if to say, "We've spoofed them all right, old boy!" It was all he could do not to burst out laughing.

The skipper took me into the control room and I spoke to some of the crew. They were accustomed to being on hush-hush work and had been personally briefed by the Colonel, who had told them nothing of the plot. To them I was the real Monty, of course, and I don't think they had any suspicions, but evidently the skipper was in the know.

The hours passed pleasantly enough and I snatched a little sleep. When I woke up dawn was beginning to break. Presently the skipper appeared and spoke in low tones to the Brigadier. What they said I couldn't hear, but both of them looked extremely grave and I sensed that something was amiss. It was only months later that I heard what it was.

The skipper said that a serious position had arisen. Owing to a fault in refuelling, or possibly to sabotage, we were running short of petrol and it was doubtful if we could reach Gibraltar. Two courses were open to us: we could come down in the sea and risk being drowned, or we could make a forced landing in Spain, in which case we should all be interned. Which course should he take?

The Brigadier was appalled, but he coolly weighed up the pros and cons. He guessed that the skipper was painting the picture a little less black than it really was. If we came down in the sea there was not much chance of our survival, while if we landed in Spain my own fate might be grim in the extreme. If

I were taken for Monty and I were subsequently found to be phoney, they might hand me over to the Gestapo. On the other hand they might discover at once that I was not Monty and the secret would be out. So the safest course was to come down in the sea and be drowned, and this was the course he decided upon.

The end of the story was that we landed at Gibraltar with enough petrol left in the tank for another few minutes' flying. Mercifully for me I was spared the agony of waiting for the engine to give the first tell-tale splutter; yet, as far as I can remember, the Brigadier, whose nerves must have been strained taut, seemed as unconcerned as if he were sitting in his arm-chair at home.

I had a shave and a wash, and as we approached the Rock I tidied myself up for Scene Two.

Just before landing there was something else to give the Brigadier a headache. Horrible sounds were heard from the back seat of the plane. Captain Moore, my second aide, was being air-sick. It was a terrible thing to happen because it struck a completely false note. Never in a thousand years would Monty, the Apostle of Physical Fitness, have had an aide who succumbed to such weakness of the flesh.

I had already seen the admirable way in which Colonel Lester dealt with unexpected difficulties, and now I was to learn what Brigadier Heywood could do.

"I'll tell him to hide himself in the lavatory until he feels better," he said tersely.

The unhappy Captain was half led, half carried to the lavatory, and locked in from the outside. And there he had to remain until he had recovered.

CHAPTER XII

I MEET HITLER'S TOP AGENTS

FAR below us I could see the famous Rock, no bigger than a mole-hill. We began to descend, skimmed the sea and made a perfect landing—two minutes late after a flight of seven hours.

As the plane taxied along the aerodrome and came to a stop, the curtain went up again. I am tempted to say that by now I had become so completely identified with Monty that I played the part by a sort of second nature, but this is not strictly true. What pulled me through were the tricks of the trade which I had learned during my long years of training and experience on the stage. I am not exaggerating when I say that throughout the Impersonation I never ceased for a moment to retain a grip of myself, to force on body and mind the complete suppression of Clifton James and so to *become* General Montgomery.

The scene before me now was strongly reminiscent of the Theatre. It was like the setting for one of those large-scale dramas which, in the old days, were staged at Drury Lane. In the background, like a vividly painted backcloth, rose the Rock. On the stage were the actors awaiting the entrance of the Leading Man. Behind were the troops, and on my left the high-ranking officers of the three Services drawn up to attention. On my right was another group and a line of cars with their drivers standing to attention beside them. There were even the 'Villains of the Piece', Hitler's agents disguised as honest Spanish workmen.

I thought of the hundreds of entrances I had made in the Theatre, some good, some bad, but all of them heavy with the feeling of stage-fright. Little had I dreamed that I should one day make an entrance like this one which would end either in disaster or in the saving of numberless lives according to the quality of my acting.

I knew that there must be not only perfection of gesture, but, what was equally important, precision in timing. So often I have seen good performances ruined by faulty timing; so often have I watched great actors and realized that their wonderful sense of timing accounted as much as anything for their success.

I should have to give the impression that I was in no hurry. With slow, easy strides I must walk towards those who were waiting for the General, greet them quietly, unconcernedly, perhaps dawdle a little, and above all take command of the situation.

I heard the Brigadier's voice behind me: "Don't forget to let as many people see you as you can manage. If you get in a jam I won't be far away."

The doors slid open and I stood on the top step. The senior officer of the Top Brass saluted. In the dead silence I gave the Monty salute, walked briskly down the gangway and over to the ranks of the high-ups.

Moving over to the other group I asked, "Is Foley here?" At once an Army Major stepped forward and saluted.

"Here, sir," he replied.

"Good," I said. "We'll get along to Government House right away."

All this may sound rather commonplace, but I had rehearsed it so often in my mind that when it actually happened it had a curious quality of unreality. It was as if everything were taking place in a dream.

Major Foley led the way to the nearest car, with Heywood following me. As I got in I said in the breezy tones of Monty: "We had a jolly good trip. The weather was as calm as a millpond."

Presently we were gliding not too swiftly through the

streets of Gibraltar, followed by Heywood in another car and a
Security Officer in a third one. I kept up a hearty conversation.

"How is the Governor?" I asked.

"He's very fit, sir, and looking forward to seeing you
again."

"It seems no time at all since we were at Sandhurst together."

"No, sir."

As I had been told, Foley was in the know. That was
inevitable. He had to organize the details of my visit, arrange
my entrances and exits and my private meetings with Sir
Ralph. But an armed escort was sitting beside the driver and
I could see that both of them had their ears cocked.

Crowds of Spanish civilians stood and watched us pass,
their faces blank and expressionless. Among them, as I knew,
were enemy agents who were ready to pass every scrap of
information back to Berlin. Our own troops seemed to be
equally curious. I could imagine them saying: "Monty! What
the hell's he doing here? Isn't he going over the top from
Dover?" I could also imagine one of the sinister-looking
Spaniards who were scowling at me suddenly whipping out
a gun and taking his chance of earning a fat reward from
Hitler.

Evidently word that Monty had arrived had flown round
quickly, for as we drove on, crowds of troops came running
from all directions, waving and shouting, "Good old Monty!"

I kept on saluting and waving back while at the same time
struggling on with my conversation with Foley. I commented
on the alterations to the harbour since I was last at Gib., and
the extensions to the docks. I even racked my brains to recall
some fragments of the Rock's past history; but all that came to
my mind was a story I had heard of some monkeys which were
treated as British subjects so far as rations were concerned.

We drove in through some big gates, turned and drew up
in front of Government House. A fair-sized crowd stood by

the gates. There was a sharp word of command and the Guard of Honour came to the Present.

I got out of the car and saluted. The doors of the building stood open, and in front of them I saw a tall, imposing figure, General Sir Ralph Eastwood, the Governor of Gibraltar.

With a smile he held out his hand. "Hullo, Monty, it's good to see you again."

"How are you, Rusty?" I replied, shaking his hand. "You're looking very fit."

"You, too, Monty. Did you have a good trip?"

"Excellent. Fine weather all the way."

In a familiar way I took him by the arm as we walked into the hall, followed by Heywood.

As Sir Ralph led me to his study I began to get carried away by my part.

"Before I forget it, Rusty," I said, "Basil sends you his salaams. I expect you've heard he's now got the 23rd Corps? You know, I believe he'll do well. He knows his job and he's keen on the new Plan."

Sir Ralph opened the door and we went in. He looked down the corridor, then shut the door carefully. In dead silence he took off his hat and sat down at his desk. To my concern he sat there and just stared at me. Then to my relief a smile spread slowly over his face. Jumping up he came over to me, his face alive with excitement, and shook me warmly by the hand.

"I wouldn't have believed it possible," he exclaimed. "You're simply splendid."

Taking me by the arm he turned me slowly round, staring at me from different angles.

"I can't get over it. You *are* Monty. I've known him for years, but you're so much like him that for a few moments I thought he had changed the plan and decided to come here himself."

"I'm glad you think I look the part, sir."

"You certainly do. But how about me? Did I sound all right?"

"I thought you were perfect."

"Do you really think so?" He seemed as pleased as a schoolboy at this piece of professional appreciation. "I felt a bit nervous to begin with. But you—you were wonderful. I've never seen acting like it. Do sit down and have a cigarette."

"I wish I could, sir, but as you know, Monty doesn't smoke. What would happen if someone looked in through the window and saw me smoking?"

Sir Ralph smiled wryly. "Good Lord, yes, I forgot. Do pull me up if I make any more mistakes like that."

He went on to explain the arrangements which had been made for me during my short stay at Government House. I was to have a private room so that I shouldn't be too much under observation. Gibraltar, he said, was swarming with people who couldn't be trusted.

He sent for Foley, and when the Major came in he said to him: "Take our friend along to his room, will you, and report back to me. See that he has everything he wants."

Foley led me up a huge, ornamental staircase to a large and comfortable room where I saw a table laid for breakfast, an armchair and a handsome writing desk. Shutting the door he leaned against it and gave a low whistle.

"Well," he said, "I thought I had seen everything, but this beats the lot."

Coming over to me he gripped my hand. "Congratulations, James, you're putting up a great show. Sir Ralph's terribly pleased. It's going over damned well."

"Do you really think so?"

"I'm certain of it."

He left me saying that breakfast would be along in a moment and that when I'd had it he would come back and take me to the Governor.

After he had gone I studied my face carefully in the mirror

and refixed my false finger which was bearing up wonderfully well. Yes, I was all right as far as my appearance went. Now that I was on the stage my nervousness had left me, and apart from a touch of weariness I felt fine.

The next thing I had to face was the man who would be bringing me my breakfast—the man who had been Monty's batman and had known him for years.

Presently I heard a knock on the door, and a grey-haired orderly entered with a "Good morning, sir". Pretending to be absorbed in some papers on the writing desk so that I was unconscious who had entered, I kept my back turned on him expecting every moment the opening shots of an awkward conversation. To my great relief he set down a plate of porridge and the coffee and left the room.

As I discovered later, the real batman had been so eager to wait on his old master that they had arranged for him to be put on special duties during my stay in Gib. I think it was a long time before he got over his disgust at this seeming piece of ill-treatment.

Having finished my breakfast, I waited for Foley to return, but ten, fifteen, twenty minutes went by and still there was no sign of him. The place was as quiet as a tomb. I could hardly stroll about Government House on my own. It was rather an alarming experience to feel myself marooned without any possibility of relief until someone chose to come along.

Having nothing better to do I looked out of the window. Outside was a square with one or two taxis, and a few loiterers leaning against a wall. Happening to glance upwards a slight movement caught my attention. I looked more closely and it dawned on me that a man in a beret was up on the roof of an adjoining building holding what looked very much like a rifle.

As far as I could see he was pointing it straight at me. I stood staring at him rather stupidly, wondering what I should do.

The room where I was had two large windows, and where

I stood, between these windows and rather far back in the room, I doubted if he could see me. But what would happen when I moved? I admit that my first impulse was to get out of the room as quickly as possible, but the next moment I remembered who I was supposed to be. In all his life Monty had never been known to show fear.

A more sensible course was to ring the bell, but to get to the bell from where I was standing I should have to cross one of the windows. Even to move might draw the man's fire. Cautiously I edged my way along until I was out of view, and then I thought how absurd the whole thing was and how I had exaggerated the danger. But the Colonel's words flashed into memory: "By the way, James, the War Cabinet mentioned danger money."

Of course, I thought, the danger is much greater than they have let on to me. They might even *expect* me to be assassinated, for what could be better from the Allied point of view than the enemy's conviction that Monty was dead and would not be directing the invasion?

Cursing myself for such qualms I stood up and had another look across the square. The man was still there and it seemed as though he couldn't miss me unless I lay flat on the floor. But I didn't fancy Foley or someone coming in and finding me grovelling on the carpet.

I remembered a play in which I had appeared years before when I had been in very much the same situation. As the Hero I had come to the rescue of a girl imprisoned by a villainous foreigner in a country house. Breaking in I had found the room empty. But the muzzle of a rifle pointed at me through the window, and I heard the Villain's grating voice, "Too late, you English swine, you've walked into the trap!"

Walking with splendid sang-froid to the window I had replied, "You think you've got me this time, Heinrich, but you're wrong." Down came the Venetian blind over the window, crash went the rifle, and I escaped unhurt.

I couldn't help smiling at the absurdity of this play, and that gave me courage to walk to the door. Passing the window I glanced upwards again and I suddenly realized that my fears were exaggerated. The man was trying to examine me through a thin telescope!

At this moment Foley came in full of apologies. Something unexpected had happened and the Governor had been held up. He was free now and ready to see me.

In his study Sir Ralph glanced at his watch and explained the next moves.

"Twelve minutes from now, you and I will take a walk in the gardens at the back of the house. You will see some scaffolding. We are having some alterations carried out on the left wing. The work, of course, is being done by native labour."

He broke off, moved to the window and looked out of it sharply.

"One of the men engaged on this work is an enemy agent!"

"Yes, sir, I guessed that."

"You guessed it? How do you mean?"

"He was looking at me through a telescope."

"The devil he was! What damned cheek!"

Sir Ralph paused and added in a different tone: "I mean, how obliging of him. This is what we want, of course. He wants to make quite certain that you're the General.

"The other point is that two prominent Spanish financiers, acquaintances of ours"—his eyes twinkled—"I would hardly describe them as friends—will be calling on Lady East-wood and myself. They want to have a look at some ancient Moroccan carpets we have here. As they pass through the gardens on their way to the house I will introduce them to you."

He glanced at his watch again. "By the way, there's a stone frieze on the garden wall. When I make some remark about it, that will be the alert signal that these chaps are due to come through the garden gates. The timing of this meeting is very important. From the enemy's point of view it has got to be one of those extraordinary coincidences. After flying 3,000 miles from England, General Montgomery decides to take a walk in the gardens of Government House at the precise moment when two high-born Spaniards come through these same gardens on their way to the house, and by pure chance the three of you come face to face. Come along, it's time we got going."

At the door he said excitedly: "Good Lord, I haven't enjoyed myself so much since I was a boy. I only wish I could act as well as you do."

"You would make a first-rate actor," I assured him.

He put on his hat and I put on my beret. He gave me a critical look, then taking me by the arm he led me along a corridor and out through a side door into the garden.

The sun blazed down from a clear sky and a pair of ring doves cooed from a nearby palm tree. We strolled slowly between the flower-beds, stopping at frequent intervals to discuss some point of horticulture. Turning down a side path we faced the left wing of the house. Looking up, I saw scaffolding and a party of workmen on the walls.

When we were close to them I said loudly: "I see you're adding to the left wing, Rusty. It's a wonderful old place. What a history!"

I noticed the man with the telescope, which was no longer in evidence, staring at me with a fearful intentness, but when I caught his eye he at once looked away and went on with his job.

The Governor replied: "Yes, Monty, the old place grows on you. Our trouble has been dry-rot, but I think we're getting rid of it at last."

We moved away and strolled between two rose-beds. Sir Ralph was a keen gardener and he had no difficulty in keeping up a glib conversation about flowers; but I who knew hardly anything about them had my work cut out to say something which sounded intelligent. I don't know how long we had been talking when Sir Ralph pointed to a wall on the top of which was a large engraved plaque representing the Battle of Trafalgar, with Nelson's flagship in the centre.

"Do you remember this frieze?" he asked. "We've had it cleaned since you were here last, but really it needs an expert to renovate it properly."

"Yes, Rusty, I do. It's a wonderful piece of work and well worth preserving."

As I said these words I heard the iron gates at the top of the garden shut with a clang. Two men were coming towards us down the centre path. Clean-shaven, in their later thirties, they were dressed in dark suits and carried hats in their hands.

Pretending not to notice them I went on talking about the frieze As the two men drew near, Sir Ralph whispered hoarsely, "Don't be nervous, James. It's a tricky moment—just keep your head."

Somewhat shaken by this warning I began to talk about the War Cabinet and Plan 303. The Governor touched me on the arm as if to caution me and I broke off abruptly, registering surprise at their approach.

Sir Ralph greeted them cordially and they bowed in the Spanish manner. I was introduced, and both of them stood looking at me with just the degree of awe and respect which they would have accorded General Montgomery. I was polite but aloof, and as I spoke I kept my hands clasped behind my back, secretly blessing Monty for this habit of his since it meant that I could keep my false finger hidden.

One of the Spaniards who looked as sinister as any spy in thriller fiction kept his snake's eyes fastened on me, while the other pretended to be interested in what Sir Ralph was saying; but I noticed that at odd moments his eyes travelled over every inch of my figure.

Looking back on the scene now, I can see them listening with ludicrous intentness to my babble of small talk about the weather, the flowers and the history of Government House.

When I judged that they had seen enough of me I said briskly: "Well, I only hope the weather holds. I have a lot more flying in front of me." And I half turned away.

At once they took their leave of me and Sir Ralph ushered them into the house. It was all over very quickly, and yet in that brief space of time the fate of those two spies and perhaps of many thousands of our soldiers was profoundly changed.

As I heard later, these Spaniards were two of Hitler's cleverest agents. Gestapo-trained and quite ruthless, they had been planted in Gib. for the express purpose of spying on me.

Some time before I met them, our own Secret Service had spread the rumour through underground channels that Monty was going to the Middle East on a highly important mission. When this news filtered through to Berlin the German High Command gave orders for the plane I was to travel in to be attacked and destroyed en route; or, if this plan miscarried, for Monty to be assassinated in Spain or Africa.

But at the last moment the Germans decided to make sure in the first place that it really was Monty and not some other General. Accordingly these two top agents who some years before had been working in Spain were flown to Berlin, where they were briefed, given faked papers and false names. After reporting to Franco's men they entered Spanish society as bankers and took up residence in Gibraltar, where they planted two of their underlings. One of these underlings got a job at the airport, the other, posing as a workman, was employed on the buildings of Government House.

When Monty arrived he was to be watched very carefully in case the English were using a double. Each spy was to put in a separate report giving every detail which he had observed, and all these reports were to be forwarded to Admiral Canaris, Hitler's Chief of Intelligence. Canaris was to decide when and where Monty was to be assassinated.

LIEUTENANT CLIFTON JAMES AND HIS WIFE

FILM DIRECTOR KENNETH ANNAKIN compliments Clifton James on his
impersonation of "Monty" in the film "Holiday Camp"

Photo Keystone

LIEUTENANT-GENERAL SIR HENRY MAITLAND WILSON (now Field-Marshal, Baron of Libya and Stowlangtoft) Clifton James continuing his role as "Monty" was received at Algiers with a Guard of Honour by Sir Henry's aides

Photo Keystone

FILM STAR JACK WARNER 'SEES DOUBLE"

All this was pretty black for me. But actually I owe my life to the Führer, for when it came to the point Hitler gave orders that Monty was on no account to be killed until it was discovered beyond doubt just where he was intending to launch his invasion. This the Germans never did discover—apart, of course, from the cross-Channel invasion—and so no attempts were made on my life.

The Spaniards must have worked pretty fast. Two hours after they left Government House, Madrid had the news that General Montgomery had arrived in Gib. and was proceeding to Africa by air. This was confirmed by our own agents in the Spanish capital.

That same evening Berlin had the news, which was also checked back by our agents in Germany. In the code message sent to Berlin was a frantic appeal: "At all costs discover nature of Plan 303. Have you any information? Very urgent."

At once the German counter-espionage department sent messages to all their embassies ordering their men to concentrate on this problem. The mysterious Plan 303 was given top priority. How the enemy spies must have cursed it!

I don't know if the complete failure of the German spy system to discover anything about this Plan aroused any doubts about my identity, but some weeks later when Monty attacked across the Channel the Germans realized how they had been hoodwinked. More dismayed than anyone were the two bogus Spanish bankers who had sent in the misleading reports.

They did not wait to be caught and put to death by the Gestapo. Crossing to La Linea they went to earth among the easy-going millions of Franco's Spain.

CHAPTER XIII

FANTASTIC TALKS WITH THE GOVERNOR

WHEN the Governor left me to show the Spaniards into the house I glanced up and saw the workman who was taking such a flattering interest in me leaning down and staring. He had given up any pretence of working. Ah well, I thought, he's doing his bit to help us win the war.

Presently I went back to Sir Ralph's study. After a few minutes the door opened and my host came in. Throwing himself into an armchair he shook with laughter.

"You and I have missed our vocations. We ought to be in the Secret Service. What do you say?"

"Do you think they had any suspicions?"

"Not the least. Did you notice their faces when you mentioned Plan 303?"

"I thought they didn't bat an eyelid."

"Oh yes they did. When you have a job like mine you have to cultivate the habit of watching men's faces. The slightest start or muscular tension is sometimes enough to give a man away."

I was with the Governor for about an hour. I suppose for all his apparent sang-froid he had felt nervous about how we should get through our act with the two Spaniards because now that it was all over, and most successfully, he evidently felt elated. And in this mood of elation he praised me so warmly that I began to feel embarrassed.

Much more clearly than I he knew the vital importance of what we were doing. Within a few hours the news of Monty's arrival at the Rock would be flying round the enemy capitals. He told me how much I had done towards shortening the war and saving the lives of thousands of our men. As he talked his imagination led him to picture me being loaded with honours and rewards from a grateful Government.

"You've done an amazing job. After this the world will be at your feet," he said enthusiastically.

In view of what actually did happen when the war was over this conversation had a touch of grim humour. However, I am not grumbling. I am very lucky to be alive today.

Sir Ralph began to explain what I was to do next.

"Your next job is at Algiers. Time is short and you're expected there as soon as possible. Your arrival at Gib. has had such a good Press that when you leave the airport I expect there'll be a full house."

He picked up the telephone receiver. "Oh, Foley, come along here with Heywood, will you?"

When the two of them came in we went carefully through the scene of departure at the airport. It was very much like the scene of my arrival—the Top Brass, the Guard of Honour, the plane's crew, all standing to attention as I got out of my car. But this time Sir Ralph would be with me, and there was to be an important addition for the benefit of any enemy agents who might be within earshot. One of them would be a certain Norwegian refugee who was working in the airport canteen.

This Norwegian and several other enemy agents in Gib. carried faked papers and had no idea that they were even under suspicion. But actually they had given themselves away by some small error and were under close observation by our own people. They were allowed to pass messages through to La Linea and from there on to Madrid; but all these messages were intercepted and read by our agents before they reached their destination.

After inspecting the officers and the Guard of Honour, I was to take Sir Ralph by the arm and stroll with him towards a point beside the Control Building. We were then to walk up and down together faking a discussion about some highly important war plans. I was to raise my voice a little so as to give the Norwegian a few tit-bits of bogus war secrets when he was within earshot. Also I was to throw my weight about and over-act to some extent for the benefit of the Spanish temperament.

When the other two had gone, the Governor said good-bye to me, although of course this was by no means the last I was to see of him. By this time I was getting used to these premature good-byes: they were all part of the looking-glass world in which things happened backwards.

Up in my room I studied my reflection in the mirror, put on my beret and came down the stairs as General Montgomery again. In the hall were my two aides with Sir Ralph. The Guard presented arms as the Governor and I got into the leading car, and we set off for the airport with an escort of armed motor-cyclists.

This time we followed a longer route. As we drove through the twisting streets I saw the same crowds of cheering Tommies and sullen Spanish civilians as I had noticed before. On the airport the bodies of Service personnel looked considerably larger. I got out of the car, bayonets flashed in the sun and a flight of Spitfires came over, dipping their wings in salute.

The usual formalities over, I took Sir Ralph by the arm and we strolled up and down, turning always when we were just under the open canteen window.

Raising my voice a little I said: "Now about these harbour defences, Rusty. I've told the P.M. that C 4 is perfectly safe. But I want the naval end tied up so that when the armour is loaded it's shipped without any time-lag."

"Yes, I understand," the Governor replied.

Pointing across the bay I went on, "If we take about three o'clock right of the cape, the engineers can alter it to fit Plan 303."

Leaving Sir Ralph's side and walking on a few paces, I shielded my eyes from the sun.

"Rusty, come here a moment. You can see the exact spot from here. Get Digby on to it at once. There's no time to waste. Understand?"

Strolling up to the open window of the canteen I let loose a final salvo of nonsense.

"I've sent a code message to Eisenhower to put Plan 303 into force. I want no belly-aching about it this end."

I can't remember what else I said. It was all arrant twaddle, and I have often pictured the scene when this precious top-secret information reached Berlin and Hitler's brain trust tried to piece it together and fit it into the general pattern of what they knew about the coming invasion. Imagine the Führer's wrath when his experts had to confess they could make nothing of it!

I was about to end this nonsensical conversation when to my surprise I noticed on the edge of the crowd the two Spanish noblemen who had come into the gardens of Government House. This was too good a chance to miss, so taking Sir Ralph's arm again I led him as near as I dared to where they were standing and this time I really let myself go.

"Rusty, this is for your ears alone. The African coast is ideal for the project, and as you know, the War Cabinet are with us all the way. The French Resistance knows all the details. Only Codes 3 and 4 are to be used by the Navy. The Air Forces will use 35 A and B for the initial softening-up. Now this affects you vitally. When the Navy sets out, all ships will be concerned with only one object: 'Prompt Side'. This is to be treated by the Admiral as a top secret."

Of course it would have been dangerous for me to be caught looking at the Spaniards, but for a split second I had a glimpse of them leaning slightly forward as if their salvation depended upon hearing what I said. It was all I could do not to burst out laughing.

We moved over to the aircraft. "Good-bye, Rusty," I said. "It has been nice seeing you again. Give my salaams to Lady Eastwood."

"Thanks, Monty, I will."

His eyes twinkled and I could almost swear he gave me the suspicion of a wink. We shook hands, the Guard presented arms, and in a few moments we took off. My last glimpse of the Governor was a stalwart figure standing at the salute with a broad grin on his face.

Well, I had completed my assignment at Gibraltar and by now the plan was becoming clear to me. On my flight out from England I had dreaded most of all the prospect of meeting high-ranking officers at close quarters, some of whom must have known the real Monty personally. I saw myself having meals at Staff Headquarters, or perhaps aboard a battleship. Although my false finger was a work of art, it would hardly bear very much close scrutiny and how could I hope to keep up a conversation on highly technical military affairs?

But I had not realized the cleverness of MI5. When it came to the point I found that things were so arranged and timed that although I was continually thrown in the path of enemy agents I always took my meals in private. And I was carefully prevented from meeting any officers who were likely to know the General personally.

When you come to think of it, all the invasion plans had been worked out in detail long before I appeared in Africa. It would have been pointless for Monty to visit any of the Commands at this juncture. All I had to do was to let myself be seen by the enemy. Certainly I ran the risk of being liquidated by some spy, but even this was less terrifying than having to discuss high strategy with our own Generals, however carefully I had been coached beforehand.

As the plane rose I thought of Colonel Lester sitting in his little room far away in Whitehall. I had read books in which master brains moved human beings about like pieces on a chessboard, but I had never expected to be a pawn in one of these fantastic games. I was now being moved to another square on the international chessboard. Looking down I could see the famous Straits of Gibraltar shrinking to the size of a bottle's neck.

I sat back and went over in my mind all that had happened in the last half-hour. Had I made any bloomers? The Brigadier sat down beside me and gave my arm a friendly squeeze.

"How do you feel?"

"Lousy. I'm trying to remember if I slipped up anywhere."

"Don't you believe it. From all I've seen and heard, you were a huge success. Of course we shan't know the results for some time, but I bet there'll be some headaches in Berlin tonight."

I tried to take his advice and relax, but it wasn't easy. Before landing at Gib. I had keyed myself up to a tremendous pitch. I'd had to remember every trick and mannerism of the man I was impersonating, every detail of the planned action I had learned at those rehearsals. For each landing and departure it had been the same. I had no idea how many more of them lay ahead of me.

While actually impersonating Monty I felt calm and sure of myself, but these off-stage intervals between the scenes were nerve-racking. It was very different from coming off the stage at the end of an Act in the theatre.

In the theatre you sat in your dressing-room with other members of the cast discussing how well or badly the show was going. All the friendly atmosphere of the theatre was there to comfort and support you. But now I had just stepped off the stage after playing one of the most dramatic scenes which any actor could hope for, and instead of the cheers or boos of the audience I could hear only the roar of the aircraft engines.

After giving me a little time to rest and relax, the Brigadier told me about the next scene. We were due to reach Algiers airport at 2.15 p.m. Algiers, he said, was a regular hot-bed of intrigue with dozens of enemy agents posing as Free Frenchmen and loyal Italian collaborators. Our Intelligence Service had already prepared the ground. Rumours had been circulated that Monty was flying to North Africa. The story was put about that he might be coming to form an Anglo-American Army to stand in readiness for an attack on the South of France which would link up with the French Resistance Movement.

These rumours had been spread all along the African coast through indiscreet telegrams, whispered reports in native bazaars, and even unguarded talk in brothels. They had travelled as far as Sicily and the Italian mainland and of course they had been reported in Berlin. It was my job now to convince the enemy spies that there was truth in these rumours and that Monty was up to something secret and highly important. In fact, that a surprise blow was being planned from the south.

We were to land at the Maison Blanche airport about twelve miles from Algiers, and our Intelligence Service had arranged that my audience should include the loyal Italian collaborators who, like our old friends the Spanish noblemen, had been briefed by the Gestapo.

A still more important stall-holder would be a French Major who had ostensibly come over to our side. A week before, he had turned up in Algiers. His papers showed him as a member of the French Intelligence Service, but as our people knew, he was really an ace enemy agent. Almost immediately he expressed a strong desire to meet Monty if he should happen to visit Algiers, and I expect he was very pleased when he was told that his wish would be gratified.

The spade-work carried out by our Intelligence people at each of the places I visited was really brilliant. Naturally the enemy would have been highly suspicious if knowledge of Monty's impending visit had been an open secret. The news was spread subtly and surreptitiously. My arrival at each place was a top secret, and yet certain selected civilians were somehow given the chance to be in the grandstand: they were allowed to pass through the cordons of guards and military police as if by acts of negligence.

To all appearances, the news was also kept secret from our own troops, but one or two obscure individuals—N.A.A.F.I. workers and others—were allowed to hear the rumour that Monty was coming. These men of course passed the news on, and in a short time everybody was talking about it—though where the rumour had originated no one knew.

Presently the skipper of the aircraft came and joined us over a cup of coffee. He pointed to a tiny island far below us and handed me a pair of field-glasses. At one end of the island I could just see what looked like a ruined tower.

When war broke out, the skipper told us, Franco sent twelve Spanish soldiers to this island with an ancient anti-aircraft gun. They had orders to fire at any plane flying over the Spanish neutral zone.

Soon after setting up their gun a Spanish plane came over. Failing to recognize it for one of their own, the A.A. crew let fly at it and by a pure fluke scored a direct hit and brought it down in flames. They were so elated by their success that they continued firing; but unhappily this was too much for the ancient gun, which burst killing the entire crew.

Once again the weather was perfect, and the Mediterranean lay below us like transparent blue glass. As we drew near the African coast the skipper remarked that it was safer to fly inland when nearing Algiers and then alter our course and approach the airport from the landward side.

"Otherwise," he explained, "everyone will start popping off at us—Americans, French, British, the whole dam lot of them."

"Any particular reason?" Heywood asked.

"No. Just fun, I suppose."

We crossed the coastline and flew inland. "I think I should

get ready now," said the Brigadier. "Another ten minutes and
we shall be landing."

All through my adventures I was constantly reminded of
MI 5's meticulous care and attention to detail. Heywood now
handed me two genuine autographed photos of Monty. You
could never tell. Although the British were in Algiers, it was a
French possession, and at the same time it was practically
being run by the American Army and Air Force. Wherever
the American Army is stationed you find American women
drivers who will stick at nothing to get the autograph of a
V.I.P. I might get into difficulties if I were blackmailed into
signing in my own handwriting, which was so different from
Monty's.

On landing at our first African station we didn't quite
know what to expect. All we knew for certain was about the
French Major and the two Italian collaborators, but we felt
pretty sure that any number of Arabs were on the look-out for
information useful to the enemy for which they would be
paid handsomely.

There had been one or two assassinations in Algiers and I
was warned that during my twelve-mile drive from the airport
there might easily be one or two sportsmen not above taking a
risk in having a pot-shot at me and qualifying for an award.
We did not know what the policy of the enemy towards Monty
might be—whether he was to be spared in the hope of discovering important information or whether he was to be
bumped off. Altogether the prospect was more sinister and
uncertain than when we had landed at the Rock.

We made our usual perfect landing, taxied across the
aerodrome and came to a stop. The doors rolled open. Prepared for anything, I stepped out on to the gangway.

CHAPTER XIV

I MEET MORE "LOYAL COLLABORATORS"

THE scene was much more colourful than at Gibraltar. I saw both a British and an American Guard of Honour and on my left a double row of French, British and American officers. Beyond them, a line of smart American cars escorted by hefty U.S. military police with motor-cycles, and finally the crew of my plane.

Only a few moments before this the crew had been at their posts, but now with the speed which comes of long practice they were drawn up in perfect order as if they had been there half an hour.

Walking down the gangway, I was greeted by members of General Wilson's Staff, after which followed the usual inspections.

A stone's throw from where I stood I saw the road to Algiers with a big polyglot crowd of civilians all waiting to catch a glimpse of General Montgomery. Standing among them, as I heard later, were the two loyal Italian collaborators who had a fine view of my arrival. They were under close observation all the time from our own people.

It was reported that one of the Italians asked an insignificant-looking Frenchman (who put in the report) what all the excitement was about, and he was told that Monty was coming to North Africa to form a great new army which would strike the soft under-belly of the Germans in the south. When the two Italians made off for Algiers the Frenchman didn't bother to follow them because he knew they were going to keep a date at the Casbar Restaurant with the French Major who was their immediate boss.

This same Major was introduced to me before I left the airfield by a Colonel on General Wilson's Staff. I have seldom met a more sinister-looking man. With his glittering dark eyes, his pale face across which ran a livid scar, and his cruel mouth, he looked, as the French say, *capable de tout*. I thought he was not above concealing a gun in his pocket and I couldn't help watching his right hand. To make things a little more difficult for him I moved so that he had the sun in his eyes.

"How d'you do, Major," I greeted him; and with a glance at his double row of ribbons: "You have seen a great deal of service. Where are you stationed?"

"At present, sare, I am in Algiers. It is a great honour to meet you."

We shook hands and he stepped back into the ranks of the officers with whom he was parading.

I had just started to walk to my car when I noticed on the far side of the airfield beyond the Control Buildings a parade of soldiers whom I seemed to have overlooked. With hands clasped behind my back I made my way towards them. But as I got nearer to them I had misgivings, for I saw that they were a detachment of the French Foreign Legion.

A French Staff Officer stepped forward and barked a word of command, whereupon they presented arms. I stood perfectly still and gave the Monty salute. There was another word of command and the detachment ordered arms and stood to attention.

The officer saluted me and looking somewhat nervous said a few words to me in French. I had no idea what he was saying, but mustering what little French I had I congratulated him on the smart turn-out of his men, saluted him and walked away.

Heywood was waiting for me with a curious expression on his face. Drawing me aside he said: "You've done it this time. That parade wasn't for you at all." As I heard later, the Legion was awaiting the arrival of some French General.

In a moment I forgot the incident, for Heywood remarked casually: "I've just had news that there may be some funny business on our way to the town. The Americans are driving us there. We could postpone our visit if you like. It's up to you."

By this time I was so much in the part of Monty that I replied curtly: "Postpone my visit? Certainly not."

We made our way to an enormous American model de luxe with a beautiful blonde American chauffeuse in a marvellously cut uniform standing by the open door. She saluted, and with all the bounce of a hard-boiled autograph hunter she began on me at once.

"Excuse me, sir——"

"Yes?"

"May I have your autograph?"

Without a smile I handed her one of my photos of Monty, remarking coldly, "I hope this one will do."

I had to behave like this because of Monty's well-known aversion to women in the theatre of war. After his wife's death he refused to have any women within miles of his headquarters in England. War, he said, was a man's job, and when on active service bachelorhood was a necessary hardship.

The fourteen powerful twin-cylindered motor-cycles which were escorting us started up with a roar, and off we went. As long as I live I shall never forget that drive from the airport to Algiers. My American escort had been warned that an attempt might be made on Monty's life and that if he were killed it would be a court-martial offence for all concerned with his safety. No troops could be spared to guard the twelve-mile route and so it was decided that the only thing to do was to drive hell for leather and hope for the best.

We shot out of the airport like a stick of rockets. Just outside, an American military policeman stood on a rostrum in the middle of the road directing the traffic. The last I saw of him was a dishevelled figure in a ditch with his box on top of him.

Down the road we tore. As we approached Algiers we came upon Arabs on donkeys, Arabs leading over-loaded camels, Arabs staggering under enormous burdens. With our sirens screaming we sent them scuttling for safety off the road.

All through this drive I kept up a Monty conversation with the Colonel—who of course was in the know—for the benefit of our lovely driver. At any moment I half expected to hear pistol shots and the crash of broken glass; and sure enough there came suddenly a loud rat-a-tat-tat on the windscreen as if someone were firing or throwing stones at us. I managed to resist an impulse to throw myself flat on the floor, and it was just as well that I did because we were only speeding through a dense swarm of locusts which happened to cross our path.

As we entered the suburbs of the town we were obliged to slow down. Crowds of natives and Servicemen lined the route, and amid cheers I saluted, waved and smiled until my muscles ached.

We climbed a steep, winding road, turned through some large gates, and pulled up at the entrance to a big mansion of white stone, General Wilson's G.H.Q. As I went in and the doors closed behind me, the curtain came down on another completed scene.

The next few days passed in a sort of recurring dream—landings, official receptions, guards of honour, bogus talks on high strategy; crowds of civilian spectators, no doubt with enemy agents among them; the streets lined with cheering troops.

"Good old Monty!"

I saluted and waved. Then back to the airport for the next lap of this curious journey.

At one airport I remember seeing Heywood coming along with an elderly civilian with a goatee beard. Dressed in a shabby black suit and carrying a big sombrero hat, he looked like a tragedian who had seen better days.

Heywood said: "Excuse me, sir. Professor Salvadore

Cerrini would take it as a great favour if you would allow him to pay his respects to you. As an archaeologist he is, of course, famous. And he's a loyal Italian," he added, seeing my dubious expression.

For a moment I wondered why I should be expected to waste my time talking to an archaeologist, but by now I knew that Heywood was not the man to do anything without very good reason. So I exchanged a few words with the Professor and when he had bowed himself out of my presence and withdrawn a few yards I turned to Heywood and said rather loudly: "The G.O.C. has been informed of my decision and the Cabinet have agreed. Operation Turtle is to be put into effect at once."

As we walked over to the plane I dropped one of the marked handkerchiefs. Heywood explained after we had taken off that Cerrini was an enemy agent with genuine fame as an archaeologist which had served him well as a 'blind'. Years later this incident was to have a curious sequel.

In another town in North Africa I was briefed by Heywood for a very short visit, the most important part of which was to be a talk with a certain Frenchwoman.

Her husband, he told me, had done very good work for us with the Resistance Movement in Paris, but was now in the hands of the Gestapo. On capturing him they had arrested his wife and given her the choice of working for them or of knowing that her husband-would die slowly in prison. The unhappy woman had with extreme reluctance accepted the first alternative and was now operating from Algiers.

When she was introduced to me I saw a tall, dark, well-dressed woman of about fifty with a face the colour of wood-ash. Remembering that Monty had no particular liking for women in the theatre of war I greeted her politely but curtly.

We exchanged a few formal words and I could not help noticing that her nerves seemed to be strained to breaking-point. Suddenly her self-control snapped. Hysterical sobs shook her whole body and then in French she began to denounce the war as the work of the Devil and me as one of war's high priests.

It was a most embarrassing situation. Not knowing how to answer her I turned abruptly away while Heywood gently led her to her car. I believe that she was intensely patriotic and at the same time very much in love with her husband. The terrible tug-of-war between these two emotions had unhinged her mind.

This was the only time that I saw Heywood disconcerted. Neither of us ever spoke of the subject again.

As the days went by I slipped into my role so completely that to all intents and purposes I *was* General Montgomery. I talked as he talked and faithfully imitated his every gesture and vocal mannerism. Even when I was alone I found myself playing the part.

Once, I remember, as I was sitting in the plane, just as we were about to land at an airport, Heywood came and stood beside me.

"All ready, Jimmy," he remarked with a smile. "How are the nerves?"

In the precise Monty tone I snapped: "Nerves, Heywood? Don't talk rot!"

"Sorry, sir," he replied with a perfectly straight face.

In a moment I realized how rude I had been and I began to apologize.

"It's extraordinary," I said. "Usually when an actor goes off the stage he at once drops the part he's playing, but with me it's the other way round. I can't get out of it. The only time I'm not Monty is when I'm asleep, and even then I dream about him."

"I quite understand," Heywood replied. "In the job you're doing it's safer always to be in your part. You never know who's watching you and you can't be too careful."

This was all very well while my job lasted, but it was now

almost at an end, and as I was soon to find out you can't *become* a great personality as I had done and then suddenly reverse the process at a moment's notice.

When, at the end of a week, I returned to General Wilson's headquarters in Algiers I certainly had the satisfaction of knowing that I had carried out my task without any serious mishap. I had been cheered by thousands of troops and honoured by some of the highest-ranking officers in the three Services, and, so far as we knew, nobody had doubted that I was General Montgomery. If this were so, there was no reason to believe that the enemy suspected anything phoney either.

But until the invasion was actually launched there was always the danger that my secret might leak out. I was now an awful skeleton in the military cupboard, a body with an embarrassing likeness to Monty's which must be stowed away like a guilty secret and conveyed under cover of darkness as if it were a corpse which might bring murderers to justice. Nor was my physical resemblance the only danger: I still *felt* like Monty and unless I were very careful I might easily arouse suspicions by continuing to act like him.

L

CHAPTER XV

WHAT TO DO WITH THE BODY?

I DROVE up to General Wilson's headquarters as Monty, in a blaze of glory, but the moment I passed through the door the glory was gone for ever.

Upstairs I changed into the uniform of a Lieutenant of the Pay Corps. My General's uniform was locked up in a case and the key of it was held by Brigadier Heywood. And while crowds of troops and civilians hung about in the road hoping for a glimpse of the great man, 'Monty' was hurried by General Wilson's aide, a Colonel, out of the back door leading from the kitchen, up a narrow lane and into a small villa standing apart. The front door of the villa was closed and bolted, and the Colonel and I were alone.

When you are *khaleef* for an hour you have at least the borrowed splendour of your position to bear you up, but when you shed the trappings of exalted rank and return to your humble station with all the backwash of the strain through which you have just passed, you certainly need all the courage and stamina you have.

When first this Colonel had seen me on my arrival from Gibraltar he had taken me to his room in G.H.Q. and behaved like a schoolboy, throwing up his hat and congratulating me with the greatest enthusiasm, telling me that 'Jumbo' Wilson would be tickled to death when he heard what a success I had been. But now when all the excitement was over he was very much a Colonel again while I was still struggling to put the Monty role behind me.

He told me that a certain Brigadier at headquarters who had planned the programme at Algiers would be coming along to see me, and that I would be sleeping at the villa until they were

146

able to smuggle 'the corpse' out of the town—which would be pretty soon because it was dangerous for me to be seen about in this part of the world.

"A batman will bring you your meals, and whatever you do, don't show your face outside the front door. Understand?"

"Yes, sir."

I began to realize what it must be like to be a hunted criminal. Your face suddenly becomes your worst enemy. It is published in the newspaper photographs and even advertised outside police stations. You try to cover it up with smoked glasses, a beard, or even by bandages over supposed injuries. But every time any stranger looks at you it seems certain that he has recognized you, and your sleep is disturbed by nightmares of police pursuits and arrest.

I expect my imagination was in a sensitive state. Too tired and overwrought to rest, I could only see again and again the scenes which had just taken place as if I were chained to my seat in a cinema.

Presently there was a knock on the door and a plump Sergeant came in. It was now about five o'clock in the afternoon and he brought me a high tea of eggs, sausages and chips.

I liked this Sergeant from the first sight of him. If it is possible to call a man 'motherly', that is the term I should use. Quick in his perceptions, he saw at once that I was all in and he did his best to help me. This villa which had been taken over by the British Army was a sort of guest house for V.I.P.s visiting General Wilson's headquarters. He must have known that I was no V.I.P. and I am sure he was intensely curious about me, but he was too well trained for his special job to ask any questions.

When I had finished my tea I heard voices outside. The door opened and I saw Heywood with another Brigadier, the famous Brigadier Dudley Clarke who founded the Commandos.

He was the man who early in the war thought of the idea

of training a gang of tough young men to strike at the enemy
behind his lines; men who would stop at nothing, and who
would use every appropriate 'un-English' means to gain their
ends. This bold plan did not appeal to the pundits at the War
Office who told him it was 'not cricket'. But he refused to take
no for an answer and was so persistent that at length he was
given a hearing. When Mr. Churchill heard about it he at once
gave orders for Dudley Clarke to go ahead.

After congratulating me on my work he told me about the
plans which had been made to get me away unobserved. On
the following afternoon an American car would be outside the
villa to take me to the Maison Blanche airport. Here I was to
board an American transport plane for Cairo. My papers signed
by himself would be made out for Lieutenant M. E. James, of
the Pay Corps, on Special Pay Duties. Someone would meet me
in Cairo and tell me what to do next. Until I was called for I
was to lie as low as a badger. On no account was I to show my
face outside.

"You look pretty fagged," was his last remark. "Try to
relax, and if there's anything you want, tell Sergeant Smith,
who's looking after you."

Heywood was even more sympathetic. "Cheer up, Jimmy,
we're all proud of you. I'll be seeing you later."

Dear old Heywood, he was the only one of them all who
seemed able to put himself in my place.

Formerly the villa had belonged to two French ladies who
had left so suddenly that they had not been able to take many
of their possessions with them. They had even left a grey and a
green parrot in the sitting-room and the Sergeant had evidently
spent a good deal of his spare time teaching them the beauties
of the English tongue. By way of cheering me up he took me
along and introduced me to them.

"Now then you two bastards," he began, "let's hear something from you."

The two parrots at once replied with language of the Old

Kent Road on a Saturday night, interspersing the swear words with odd bits of lady-like French.

"Talk English, you silly bitches," the Sergeant shouted. "I don't want any parleyvoos from you!"

The grey parrot seemed friendly enough and allowed me to scratch her head, but the green one, who was called Lizzie, had a look in her eye which I didn't fancy, and when I tried to scratch her she made a vicious peck at my finger.

This bird, the Sergeant told me, was amazingly quick at picking up words, but parrot-like she would usually forget them just as quickly unless they were repeated. Looking back on it later, I realized that this was a clear warning to a man in my ticklish position. Had I known what might happen I would never have come near those wretched birds.

But that evening, wandering aimlessly about the villa unable to read or to rest, some wicked sprite tempted me to visit the parrots again and try to get them to talk. I tried my hardest in English, but not a word could I get out of them. At last in exasperation I swore at them, whereupon Lizzie replied with a string of the foulest oaths I have ever heard. If words mean anything to a parrot she had evidently taken a strong dislike to me.

It is absurd to take offence at a parrot. I can only plead that my nerves were more than a little on edge.

"Don't you talk to me like that," I snapped. "I'm Monty."

Lizzie gave a hideous squawk.

"Monty," I hissed, bending down close to the cage. "Do you hear? Monty!"

The bird stood motionless with her eyes glittering. Without warning she let out a piercing whistle which increased the throbbing in my head. I made for the door.

Just as I was going out Lizzie screamed again, and then that miserable bird began to shriek "Monty!"

I stood there in terror. Perhaps I was in a mood to

exaggerate the dangers. All the same, if Sergeant Smith were to hear what the parrot was shrieking he could hardly fail to wonder what was the cause of it. And the disturbing fact remained that even without my General's uniform I still looked very much like Monty.

My fears became almost panic when the Sergeant came along the passage. I managed to head him off, and then I went back to the aviary and considered what I should do.

For months I had succeeded in keeping my mouth shut to friends and acquaintances—even to my own wife. And now I had opened it—to a parrot! It only remained for Brigadier Clarke to come along and hear my indiscretion broadcast from a bird-cage to land me in the guard-room.

Lizzie looked at me evilly as if she perfectly understood all this.

I'll try kindness first, I thought. Contorting my face into a winning smile I cooed, "Hullo, Polly, pretty Poll, good old Lizzie."

This and many other endearing expressions were greeted in silence, and with some relief I remembered having heard the Sergeant say that Lizzie was as quick to forget words as to pick them up. But just when I was beginning to feel somewhat reassured there came the piercing whistle and "Monty! Monty! Monty!" in a shattering crescendo.

I contemplated violence, but my tormentor seemed to see the futility of this even more quickly than I did, for she jumped up and down on her perch as if to express derision.

I considered opening the cage and pushing Lizzie out of the window, but on second thoughts I didn't relish the prospect of her squawking "Monty!" in the streets of Algiers and then being captured in a blaze of publicity. So at last I returned to my own room and dozed off.

After what seemed only a few minutes I was awakened by the Sergeant with a cup of tea.

From the next room there came a piercing whistle and

then: "Monty! Monty!" I looked at the Sergeant and he looked at me.

"That little bitch is pretty quick in the uptake," he remarked casually.

I felt my throat going dry as I tried to think of something to say.

"This Monty how-d'y-do is supposed to be hush-hush. The mess orderly and I were talking about it yesterday and I suppose Liz must've heard us."

I gaped at him.

"Trust her to contravene the Official Secrets Act."

He picked up my empty cup, gave me a curious look and went out. To this day I don't know if he guessed my secret and was saying all this to reassure me.

After an almost sleepless night I had some breakfast, and then wondered how on earth I could pass the next six hours. Upstairs there was a room with a small balcony outside it. I went and sat in the sun, admiring the lovely view of the town and harbour. But at eleven o'clock the Sergeant showed in Brigadier Clarke. I thought he was looking rather stern.

As soon as the Sergeant had left the room he said sharply, "Did I see you up on that balcony just now?"

"Yes, sir. I sat out there to get some air."

"I told you on no account to show yourself outside this villa. Don't do it again. All the work you have done might be ruined if someone spotted you."

The reason for these strict precautions was that it was an open secret that mysterious visitors stayed at the villa. No doubt enemy agents kept an eye on it, and if one of them happened to see someone who resembled Monty and yet was *not* Monty, the cat would probably be out of the bag.

He gave me my papers and an Army pass to travel by air to Cairo. I suppose Cairo was chosen as being the one town which was big enough to swallow me up without a trace. Once again I was given no hint as to what would happen to me when

I got there or who would meet me. But by this time I had grown quite accustomed to being shot into the unknown like a refugee.

While we were talking, Heywood came in to bid me a warm and friendly good-bye. I felt horribly alone when he had gone and I began to see how much I had come to rely on him now that he was no longer to be at my side.

At three o'clock a big, closed American car stood outside, and coming down to the hall I saw a strange Army Major as heavily armed as a character in a thriller.

"Lieutenant James?" he asked.

"Yes, sir."

In a low voice he said: "I'll open the car door. Dash straight into it. Keep your head down and blow your nose. Is that clear?"

A few moments later I grabbed my hold-all and literally dived into the car. The door slammed, the Major got in beside the driver, and we were off.

CHAPTER XVI

D-DAY SETS ME FREE

The Major bade me good-bye as I got out of the car and walked to the huge reception office on the aerodrome. I was quite accustomed to the Maison Blanche by this time. Everything was 100 per cent American. American personnel, American aircraft, loud-speakers booming in broad American accents.

All through my adventures complete strangers were constantly looming up and delivering strange letters or verbal messages. I was not at all surprised when a young Captain came up to me and presented me with a sealed envelope which he said he had been told to deliver to me. Opening it, I discovered £E20 provided by the thoughtful Brigadier.

After a quarter of an hour the loud-speakers began booming, "Passengers for Zero-one-Zero, take your places in Bay Six."

This referred to me. In Bay 6 I found a big American transport plane in which I managed to get a seat at the back. Ten minutes later the engines roared and we were off on our journey to Cairo. Since we had eight hours before us I had plenty of time to study my fellow passengers.

The first thing that struck me was the strange dress worn by some of the American Air Force men. It was so peculiar that I thought they must be civilians until I heard them talking in Service jargon. They wore nondescript trousers and zip-fastener wind-cheaters, and in their pockets they carried flat caps. All the luggage that one of them seemed to possess was a pair of pliers stuck in his belt. Two others sat near me and for eight hours neither of them spoke a word. They just sat there like ruminative cows, stolidly chewing gum.

For the rest there was a collection of Australian, British, French and American Servicemen with one or two civilians. An Aussie soldier began to give us a running commentary on the North African battlefields beneath us. He had been right through the campaign and his vivid narrative helped to take my mind off my own problems.

How I had looked forward to the moment when the Impersonation was over and I could sit back and relax, and how different it was from what I had imagined! If the enemy were really clever, I might be under observation even now, and certainly when I landed at Cairo there would be enemy agents waiting for me. Only those who have carried international secrets know how heavily they can weigh a man down. How much longer should I have to bear the burden of secrecy?

At 10.45 p.m. we were told to fasten our safety belts and in a short time we landed on the Cairo aerodrome. Crowds of people of many nationalities pressed round me.

After handing in my papers at the Control Building I looked round for someone who might be there to meet me, but I saw no one at all. I found a seat tucked away in a corner and sat there wondering what on earth I should do if nobody came. I knew absolutely nothing of Cairo and wherever I went I should be asked for my pass and my other papers. All I had with me was a letter saying that I was on Special Pay Duties. If I were questioned about these mysterious duties what could I say? Any story I concocted would at once be checked up and proved to be false.

As time went by I grew more and more anxious. The reception office was beginning to empty now and two military policemen eyed me with obvious suspicion. If no one turned up in the next quarter of an hour, I said to myself, I would ask the way to the nearest Y.M.C.A. and try to get a bed there.

I was just getting up to do this when a tall, handsome Major of the Guards came quickly up to me with his hand out.

"Hullo, are you James?" he asked. "I'm awfully sorry I'm

late, but we didn't get the message from Algiers about your coming until an hour ago. Here, give me your hold-all, I expect you're feeling pretty well fagged out. The car's outside and I've got a nice dinner waiting for you."

As we walked out of the building we must have appeared a strange couple: a weary-looking Lieutenant of the Pay Corps with a Major of the Guards carrying his hold-all like a batman. I thought of the cartoon about our democratized Army showing a General lying under a car which has broken down and his driver smoking unconcernedly at the wheel.

Our car moved off and the Major said: "I'd better introduce myself. I'm Terence Kenyon."

"It's very kind of you to look after me like this, sir," I began, but he interrupted: "Forget the 'sir'. While you're in Cairo you're going to stay with me as my guest. I'm Terence to you, and I'll call you Jimmy. How's that?"

He went on to tell me that he worked in an Army office in Cairo and that his job was to welcome anyone who had been on a special job.

"I have no idea what you've been doing and I don't want to know," he told me. "Our instructions from General Wilson's headquarters are that you've done a good job of work and that you're to lie low in Cairo, have a good rest and return home in a few weeks' time."

This relieved me considerably because I had been rather nervous of having to explain myself with some faked story. Terence was an excellent host. He chattered away about life in Cairo, told me funny stories, and in a very short time, as it seemed, I was sitting in an armchair in his comfortable flat.

My stay in Cairo was as pleasant as he could make it, but after the first day or two I longed for home. The heat, the squalid poverty of the fellaheen, the flies which crawled in swarms over the sticky faces of small boys and girls, the sickness and inertia—all combined to make an unpleasant impression.

Thieving was widespread. Terence told me of an officer who lost literally everything he possessed. This vice even spread to domestic pets. Some weeks back Terence's bull-terrier bitch had had a litter of puppies. A pair of apes belonging to the man next door stole the litter and climbed a tree, each ape with an armful of pups!

One night I woke up with a terrible toothache. Next morning it was no better. As I was very run down and unaccustomed to semi-tropical heat I suppose there was reason for it. When I told Terence about it he sent me to an Army dentist, but on the way there I suddenly remembered my rather alarming experience with the dentist in Leicester. Evidently my tongue was unreliable under gas, and now was hardly the time to take any risks with it. So I turned back home again. But next day the toothache was worse, and at length I was driven into visiting the dentist, an overworked, elderly man who told me that I should have an official authorization which I hadn't got. He also told me that I had an abscess and that he couldn't give me a local anaesthetic.

I suppose if I had been cast in the heroic mould I would have gone away again and endured the pain, but as it was I agreed to return later in the day. Arriving early I read the journals in the waiting-room, trying hard to keep my mind off the subject of the Impersonation.

Twenty minutes later the tooth was out. I recovered consciousness to find the dentist and the doctor regarding me with very curious expressions.

"Did I say anything when I was under?" I blurted out.

"You certainly did," the doctor replied with a sardonic grin. "In fact you began to give us quite a lecture."

"What on?"

"How to improve our busts in a six weeks' course of treatment."

Since there was a large Pay depot in Cairo I was almost

certain to know some of the personnel. I avoided public places as far as I could and I spent much of my time in gardens on the banks of the Nile. But one day lunching at the Ghezirah Club the thing happened which I had tried so hard to avoid. We had just ordered coffee when a voice exclaimed, "Hey, James, fancy seeing you here!"

I quickly looked the other way and tried to hide my face; but it was no good. I knew that voice only too well. It belonged to an officer whom I had come to know in the Pay Office at Leicester, one of those camp followers of Thespis who are always talking about theatrical people they have never met and using stage expressions in the wrong way. Even in Leicester I had tried to avoid him, but here in Cairo he was doubly unwelcome. He came over to our table with a broad, confident grin.

"Well, well, who would expect to see the great Clifton here," he began in his brassy voice. "What on earth are you doing in the Gorgeous East?"

"Oh, this and that," I replied as distantly as I could. But he was not to be put off.

"What's the news from dear old London? How are all the shows doing, eh?"

"You must excuse me," I replied. "I had a tooth out yesterday and I find it very painful to talk."

My unwelcome acquaintance tried to take this as a joke, but Terence coming to my rescue looked exceedingly grave and told him that the dentist had broken my jaw in extracting a molar with very long roots. Even then we had great difficulty in getting rid of him.

I made a resolution then and there never to go to the club again, but the trouble was that wherever I went I might run into people who had known me in England. Leicester was one of the biggest Pay Corps depots in the Kingdom and thousands of men passed through it before being posted abroad. Not only this, since I had disappeared suddenly with no explanation

to anyone I was bound to be an object of curiosity. In fact in
Leicester I must have been a wide topic of conversation.

One day I was waiting for Terence in Shepheard's Hotel
when the manager hurried past me and stuck a news bulletin
on the notice-board. Quickly a crowd gathered round to read
it. I asked someone what it was all about and he replied: "The
Invasion has started. We're well inland and giving them hell."

He threw his hat in the air and shouted "Whoopee!", whereupon those round him began slapping each other on the back
and cheering.

I walked away from the board in great excitement wondering how much my own effort had helped in this initial success.
It was not until after the war was over that I was told how the
deception had assisted in deceiving the enemy and drawing
away Rommel's armoured divisions.

One day about a fortnight later Terence told me that he
had had instructions to get me home by air almost at once.
While I was in his office watching him make out my papers,
an A.T.S. officer whom I had met before came in and asked me
if I would take an important package and post it for her in
England. Thereupon she handed me a parcel about the size of a
big square biscuit tin.

"It has no visible address on it," she explained. "As soon as
you land, tear off the outer covering and you'll find the address
on the inside."

I was too well trained in secrecy by this time to ask any
questions.

"It's a Top Secret and extremely important," she added.
"Guard it with your life, won't you?"

What could I do but give her my promise.

In the evening I said good-bye to Terence with genuine
regret. He had been a wonderful friend to me, had never asked
me a single question about my recent doings and had done all
he possibly could to make me happy and comfortable. A
quarter of an hour later I reported to the Air Force office,

After having my papers checked I sat down and waited for transport to the airport. The clerk looked up and said curtly, "You'd better wait outside with the others."

As if a press-button had been touched I stood up and with hands clasped behind me I barked: "You will be respectful to a commissioned officer. When you address an officer you will say 'sir'."

He sat there gaping at me. "Stand to attention!" I snapped. At once he got up and stood to attention looking distinctly scared. Only when I turned and left him did I realize that I had spoken in the exact manner of General Montgomery.

There was no doubt that I had changed in some curious way and had cultivated a genuine feeling of superiority. Since shedding my General's uniform I had tried hard to get rid of this, but more than once while staying with Terence I had seen a peculiar look on his face and I had realized that I had slipped back into the Monty role. It is true that earlier on I had felt timid and diffident at times, but as soon as I heard the news of our successful landing in Normandy, relief and confidence flowed into me and the Monty Manner came to me only too easily.

My flight from England as General Montgomery had been fantastic. My return flight was no less fantastic, but in quite a different way.

The first fellow travellers to meet my eye were a couple of disconsolate-looking Privates of the D.L.I. who were sitting on the ground with their backs to a wall. I squatted down beside them with a bright "Good evening", at which they eyed me apathetically. One of them replied " 'Ow do", the other muttered "B—— Farook". They looked completely brainless and almost identical. In my mind I nicknamed them Tweedle-dum and Tweedledee.

Presently a taxi drew up and spilled out a couple of naval officers each of whom clutched a bulging suitcase. They embraced one another for support, moaned out a verse of a bawdy song and were propelled into the office by an obliging military policeman. Five R.A.F. men made up our complement of ten.

An Air Force truck came along to convey us to the airport. Tweedledum and Tweedledee clambered in, followed by the naval officers who were hoisted aboard by the driver and the military policeman rather like milk churns on to a farm lorry. Both of them at once went to sleep. On being woken up at the airport they were in a smouldering temper which burst into flames when they were told in the checking-room that their bags were over-weight. In true naval fashion they cursed the N.C.O. in charge, but the latter stuck to his guns and refused to give way.

Then an extraordinary thing happened. Suddenly snatching up their suitcases they ran to the plane with the N.C.O. running after them. Their attitude was so threatening that on nearing the aircraft the N.C.O. thought better of it and ran back to the Control Building for help. Quickly the naval men opened their cases and decanted a quantity of contraband into their overcoats which they folded up and thrust under the seats of the plane. Before long the N.C.O. arrived with a haughty-looking officer and the Navy with its baggage was conducted back to the Control Building.

Having followed this real life drama thus far I put my money on the Navy. The bags were weighed again and found to be *under* weight. The officer gave the unfortunate N.C.O. a most unmerited 'rocket' and the Navy made a triumphal return with flags flying. In silent admiration the rest of us watched these two heroes repack their cases at leisure with about £100-worth of contraband apiece and then make themselves comfortable for the journey.

As I boarded the plane I saw on my left a big heap of parcels and mail-bags with one or two R.A.F. men settled on top of the heap like moles. On the other side six iron bucket-seats were placed close together. With my precious parcel under

CLIFTON JAMES AS "MONTY" in a scene from the Chilham Castle, Kent, Pageant in 1946

Photo P.A./Reuter

CLIFTON JAMES TODAY

my arm I wedged myself into one of these seats, but it was impossible to get into a comfortable position.

From the conversation I overheard I realized with some dismay that we were about to take off in an ancient Dakota. The best opinion seemed to be that we had a fifty-fifty chance of getting home without crashing.

The outer doors closed, and after a pause the door opened which led to the navigator's cabin. A fair-haired, middle-aged pilot stood in the doorway and behind him I saw another elderly officer with glasses. With dark rings under their eyes and pale, drawn faces they looked more like winners of a non-stop dancing competition than R.A.F. pilots.

"Now, you chaps," the first one began in a weary voice, "we're just going to take off. There'll be one stop in the morning before we reach Gib. This kite's got no guns, so if we're attacked just hang on. If we come down in the Drink you'll find a hand-axe in her tail. One of you get hold of it and hack your way out."

The officer behind him added: "And somebody release the dinghy. It *may* float."

The first one yawned: "Sorry if I seem a bit sleepy. Neither of us has had any sleep for five nights. We've been flying backwards and forwards for a week between India and Ceylon —without any kip."

He swayed dizzily against the door. "Don't any of you touch the emergency door-handle on the right. Last week some B.F. leaned on it and two chaps fell out."

He gave us a wintry smile, yawned and disappeared with his companion. The explanation was that the Invasion had started and such pilots and planes as were not involved in it were working overtime.

After the silence which greeted this cheering news, Tweedledum croaked, "Eh, ba goom, I was leaning on t'bloody handle all the time 'e was talkin'." Tweedledee merely grunted "B—— Farook".

M

One of the naval men muttered irritably: "Emergency handle my foot. If they don't hurry up and take off we'll chuck these silly old bastards out and fly the damn thing ourselves."

"Eh, I 'ope not. We'll never get 'ome if you do," said Tweedledum.

Up jumped the naval officer. "Hey, what was that?" he shouted angrily. "Stand up so I can see you."

Tweedledum and Tweedledee gaped at him stupidly and slowly rose to their feet. The naval officer took a step towards them, but at this moment the engines started so sulkily that drunk as he was he had qualms about whether we should ever leave the ground. He passed a trembling hand across his brow and stumbled back to his seat.

Tweedledee said "B—— Farook" and sat down. Tweedledum followed his example.

CHAPTER XVII

FANTASTIC FLIGHT HOME

THAT night I found it difficult to sleep. With the iron seat digging into my back, my knees wedged against the seat in front of me and my Top Secret parcel sticking into my ribs, it was impossible for me to get into a comfortable position. At times I was very much tempted to throw the wretched parcel out of the window and only a high sense of duty prevented me from doing this.

All through the night we droned on, every now and again striking an air-pocket and falling like a celluloid ball in a shooting-gallery. As dawn broke I could see the desert far below us stretched like a Wilton carpet.

Round about 7.0 a.m. we came down and landed at Castel Benito. It was a desolate spot. Beyond the runway were a few huts and tents. The heat was already terrific.

We must have looked a bedraggled party as we made our way to some water-taps sticking out of the sand. Depositing my parcel close beside me, I stripped to the waist, had a good wash and began to shave. The two naval men were doing the same thing at the next tap.

Suddenly one of them began to jump up and down, slapping himself and using the most lurid language, and at the same moment I felt a sting on my stomach. Looking down I saw a Commando contingent of huge ants swarming up my leg. Beating them off as best I could I finished my shave in record time and went to the mess tent where an Italian waiter, a prisoner of war, served us with an extremely greasy breakfast and some black coffee. Our pilot and navigator with their tired, drawn faces looked literally at the last gasp. It was a

wonder to me they had managed to get us even this far without
disaster.

We passengers all drifted back to the plane, took our
seats and settled down for the flight to Gibraltar. After
sitting there for half an hour the Navy began to grow
restless.

"What in hell do those two so-and-so's think they're
doing?" one of them growled. "Why can't we get cracking?"

Another ten minutes went by and they both decided to go
and see what was happening. I followed them to a tent, inside
which we found the pilot and the navigator sprawled over a
table sound asleep with their heads buried in their arms. An
R.A.F. Sergeant was shaking them and shouting, "Wake up,
sir. Come along, sir, you're late already," while the Italian
waiter was gesticulating and exclaiming, "*Sapristi!*"

The two naval men pushed the Sergeant aside, shook the
unhappy pilot and navigator like terriers shaking rats, stood
them up and slapped their faces. The two sleepers moaned a
little and started to go to sleep again, their heads lolling like
those of sawdust soldiers. One of the naval men took a jug
of water and flung it in their faces, but even this did little to
rouse them.

We stood there looking at the poor devils and wondering
what would happen next. It seemed as if we should have to
apply for a couple of replacements to take us back to England.
With the Invasion now in full swing and every transport plane
in full use for ferrying troops and stores, I suppose we were
lucky to get any aircraft at all. But with an unconscious crew
it was about as much use as a flying carpet without the magic
word to make it fly.

Once again the resourcefulness of the Navy came to our
rescue. One of the officers sent the waiter for a siphon of soda
water, and when it was brought he pushed the nozzle into the
pilot's nostril and squirted. The poor chap choked and coughed
and opened his eyes. A few more squirts and he was awake at

last. The navigator received similar treatment and he too was dragged back from the Land of Nod.

"What's happening?" the pilot asked querulously. "Can't a chap have five minutes' rest without being drowned in soda water?"

"We'll drown you in something else if you don't get cracking," said the naval man.

"Hell!" exclaimed the pilot feebly. "Are we crossing the Line, or what?"

"You'd better cross your fingers in case we stop treating you like a little brother and get tough with you," was the reply.

Still bickering, we made our way back to the plane and at last took off.

Some time later I was looking down at the Rock. Opening the inter-connecting door the pilot called out, "Get your belts on, it's a bit bumpy over Gib."

This was an understatement. The old Dakota bucked like a bronco and once or twice dropped so far that it felt like falling down a well.

We landed, and soon I was standing on the identical spot where I had said good-bye to Sir Ralph Eastwood. In place of the Governor, a red-faced Major strode up to us and eyed us with disfavour.

"Now then," he cried, "don't hang about here. Come on, follow me—and make it snappy."

"Who the hell are you talking to?" asked the Navy. As I discovered later, these two naval officers had been rescued from a wrecked submarine and their nerves and tempers were none too good.

The Major's face turned a shade redder. "Cut that out," he snapped. "I'm in charge here. Come on, get a move on."

Growling like a seedy dog the naval man followed him to the Control Building. The D.L.I. were delighted to see the Navy worsted for once.

" 'E's got that stinker taped," chuckled Tweedledum under his breath.

"Aye," replied Tweedledee, and he added his usual signature-phrase.

After our papers had been' checked the Major lined us up and reading out our names from a list, allotted us our billets. We were to wait until a plane was ready to take us on to England. Apparently the authorities had at last awakened to the fact that our crew were in a state of somnambulism and had given orders for them to be given a short rest.

Having had little sleep ourselves, we passengers were hardly less weary, and hearing that my billet was in the Bristol Hotel I asked the Major if there was any chance of transport.

"Who the hell do you think you are?" he snorted. "A Field Marshal? Make your own way on foot."

At once I drew myself up, clasped my hands behind my back and was just about to snap out something in the Monty Manner when one of the naval men got in front of me.

"If you don't get us transport," he said, "I shall put in a complaint to the Naval Commander-in-Chief. You can do what you like about it." And he turned away.

The Major didn't like this at all, and after some blustering to save his face he promised to get us transport right away. While awaiting its arrival we went along to the canteen.

Leaning against the counter I heard a voice with a foreign accent: "Please? What can I get, sir?" I looked up and saw a middle-aged man with white hair, very bushy eyebrows and piercing grey eyes.

Tweedledum said, "You're a long way from 'ome, chum."

"Many miles," was the reply. "I am from Norway."

Something connected up in my tired mind and I turned quickly away. I wondered what he would have said if I had asked him how Plan 303 was getting on.

A lorry arrived at last and we all got in. It took us through those same streets where crowds had lined the route on my departure from Gib. only a week or two before.

My room at the Bristol Hotel proved to be a cheerless, bare place with an oleograph of Queen Victoria hanging on the wall and two camp beds, on one of which an Army officer lay snoring. I lay down on the other bed and closed my eyes, but I couldn't sleep a wink.

I began to think of lunch, and suddenly I remembered that only 30 piastres remained of my £E20. How could I pay for lunch or anything else? What would happen to me when I got back to England with nothing in my pockets?

Staring across the room I saw on the opposite wall a framed notice. I can't remember the wording, but it said in effect that anyone in monetary difficulties could change his money at the Royal Army Pay Corps office. Some wag had scrawled underneath it, "If you haven't any money to change, pop your dentures."

This was all very well, but if I went to the Pay Office I might easily run into some officer I had known in Leicester who would ask me awkward questions. I was still under an oath of secrecy and I meant to keep this oath until MI 5 released me from it. With my Top Secret parcel under my arm—a parcel I was beginning to detest—I slipped out of the hotel and then wondered what to do next.

I could hardly go to Government House and ask Sir Ralph for the loan of a couple of pounds. Eventually I enquired from a Corporal in the Signals the way to the Chief Security Officer in Gib.; for I knew that he, at any rate, would have been in the know about the Impersonation.

At the police-station in Main Street I asked the military policeman at the door if I could see the Security Officer. He looked at me in astonishment.

"Sorry, sir, nobody can see him without an appointment. Can I help you?"

"This is a very personal matter," I explained. "It's really important."

"I'm afraid you'll have to tell me what it is."

"Rot!" I snapped, clasping my hands behind my back. "You will tell him that I wish to see him at once."

He looked startled. In a different tone he said: "All right, sir, I'll do my best. If you're willing to risk it I'll take a chance on it and ask him."

I followed him upstairs to a room where some more military police were waiting. Asking me to leave my precious parcel in his charge, he knocked on the Chief's door and went in. Presently he came out again breathing rather heavily.

"I wouldn't care to be you, sir, if your business isn't important," he confided in a low voice.

He knocked at the door again, a deep voice growled "Come in!" and in I went.

I found myself in a barely furnished office facing an Army Colonel who was seated at his desk. He was one of the fiercest-looking men I have ever seen, with a huge bristling black moustache.

"Well?" he began, glaring at me. "What do you want?"

He looked so threatening that I was petrified.

"Come on, speak up," he went on.

"Well, sir, it's about money. I haven't any, and I thought perhaps you could——"

"No money!" he roared. "Can't you read the notices?"

"Yes, sir, but——"

"If you want money, go to the Pay Office. Now get out!"

Instead of leaving his office I drew myself up and looked at him almost as fiercely as he had looked at me. For a few moments we stared at each other in silence. In clipped accents I said, "I think you are making a mistake."

I saw amazement, anger, incredulity cross his face in rapid succession. He continued to stare at me, and presently his face relaxed and broke into a smile.

"Good Lord! My dear chap—now I know who you are. Why on earth didn't they send me a message from Cairo that you were on your way here?"

He got up and shook my hand. "What a marvellous show you put up! I shall never forget it. I hear the Governor is still chuckling about it."

Over a cigarette he asked, "Well, what can I do for you?"

I explained that I had no money and dared not go to the Pay Office where I might meet someone who would recognize me.

"Of course, my dear boy. How much do you want?"

He took ten pounds out of his safe and handed them to me. "Will this be enough?"

"Plenty, thank you, sir. It's very kind of you."

"Not at all. Delighted."

We chatted for a while about the Impersonation and he gave me some news about how my bogus Top Secrets had flown round the enemy capitals. When I got up to go he came out of his office and stood for a moment with his hand on my shoulder before saying good-bye to me, as if I had been a life-long friend. This was not the first time I had noticed that fire-eaters are usually warm-hearted men.

When he had gone back into his office five military policemen all stood and stared at me in amazement.

"Did you hear what I heard, or am I dreaming?" asked the one who had got me in. " 'It's been jolly nice meeting you! The very best of luck to you!' "

Turning to me he added, "Well, sir, I reckon you must have the magic touch."

Picking up my parcel I returned in triumph to the hotel, where I had lunch which from its taste might have been monkey soup and goat stew. In the evening I rejoined my travelling companions in the canteen and stood them all drinks. I looked so jaunty that one of the Navy asked me what her name was.

Presently our pilot and navigator appeared yawning and rubbing their eyes, and we tramped out to our ancient machine.

We took off well enough and for many hours we chugged along without mishap. At length dawn broke and I saw that it was pouring with rain. To everyone's dismay one of the engines began to splutter.

Our pilot's head appeared in the open doorway. "Very sorry, you chaps, I've tried to switch over to my spare tank but the juice won't come through. Better get your Mae Wests on as quick as you can."

Most of us stood up and began wrestling with our safety belts, the naval men cursing the Air Force in horrible language. Having got mine on I glanced behind me and saw the D.L.I. sitting motionless.

"Didn't you hear what he said?" I asked them. "Aren't you going to put on your Mae Wests?"

"Noa," said Tweedledee, "we doan't believe in them affairs. If we're going in t'water me and my pal'll swim together, etc." Apparently he held the Egyptian Sovereign responsible even for an air-lock in the petrol feed-pipe.

I looked out and saw the rugged cliffs of Cornwall bouncing up and down like crazy stage scenery. This is the end of my adventure, I thought. I've been through all this only to finish up in Davy Jones's Locker.

It seemed to me that whole hours passed, though I suppose it was only a few minutes, while we bobbed about in our mad flight. Then suddenly to our immense relief the engines roared and we climbed steadily. Looking down I saw that we had passed over the cliffs and were making a steady course inland. At about half-past six in the morning we landed in pouring rain.

It was a small, deserted R.A.F. aerodrome somewhere in the heart of Devonshire. As we got out not a soul was in sight, but presently an N.C.O. came up and put a sentry on the plane. Clutching our luggage we trotted through the downpour to the Control Building which was about half a mile away. The rain was so heavy that we were wet through long before we got there.

I couldn't help comparing this ignominious return with my magnificent departure from Northolt. A taggle of displaced persons fleeing from the wrath of Hitler could hardly have looked more woebegone.

When we reached the Control Building a very young and sleepy officer of the R.A.F. appeared with an overcoat over his pyjamas, and then there followed a scene which for me personally was as trying as any that I had gone through.

"Look here," he began, "we only got your signal a few minutes ago and we have no clearance for you to land here."

Ignoring an uncomplimentary remark from one of the naval men, he went on: "I don't know who the hell you are or where you've come from. The whole thing's completely out of order. I've no authority for your landing. You'd better go on and land somewhere else."

Tired, hungry, soaked to the skin, none of us could think of what to say until the other naval officer let out a stream of oaths which would have done credit to an Oriental.

Stung by this broadside, the Air Force officer lost his temper, and next moment we were all arguing, protesting and swearing, except for Tweedledum and Tweedledee who seemed to be incapable of grasping what was happening. At length our pilot and navigator appeared and drew the angry officer aside. I don't know what passed between them, but after a lengthy wait, an orderly came to tell us that the Medical Officer was ready to see us. I followed the others and waited for my turn to go in. When it came I saw a grey-haired, portly Captain of the R.A.M.C. with a row of medal ribbons, probably a Regular officer, sitting at a table with furrowed brow. In front of him on the table was a list of our names.

He glanced up. "Your papers, please."

I handed him my military identity card and the papers showing that I had been abroad on Special Pay Duties.

Frowning, he said, "No, I mean your medical papers."

Not realizing what he was talking about I blurted out:

"Medical papers? I haven't any. These are the only papers I've got."

He sat up with a jerk. "I have a busy day in front of me. Please don't waste my time."

Leaning forward he said slowly and emphatically, "I want to see your papers showing that you were inoculated against malaria, blackwater fever, dysentery, and so on before you left England."

In a flash I saw the jam I was in. I had no medical papers. Had Colonel Lester slipped up for once? On reflection I realized that everyone without exception had to be inoculated before going abroad. Even Royalty were not exempt. But I was the one man in ten million who had *not* been inoculated, and I could hardly explain why.

What had happened, I imagine, was this. Originally they had meant to send me only to Gibraltar, but at the last moment it was decided to expand the whole plan of deception and send me farther afield. Also, they had pursued the plan of letting a bare minimum into the secret even if it entailed difficulties when the plan of deception was finished. If I had been medically examined and subjected to the usual programme of inoculations, my medical papers would have been referred to my unit, and various medical officers and orderlies who were not in the know might have suspected something unusual. Evidently it had been decided to break the medical regulations and leave me to deal as best I could with any ensuing difficulties.

The M.O. was rapidly becoming exasperated. It was extremely awkward for me because obviously I had to give him some sort of answer.

"Well, sir," I said, "as a matter of fact I was not inoculated before I went abroad. I've been on a secret assignment."

He got up and began pacing up and down the room. Coming to a halt in front of me he said: "Then the position is, having come from Cairo and the Middle East without being inoculated, you are probably a carrier of a number of infectious diseases. This is a serious matter and I'm afraid you'll have to go into quarantine."

"Yes, sir."

"There's something rather improbable about your story. To be frank with you, I don't believe it. I shall have to get in touch with Pay Corps headquarters in Leicester and find out more about you."

It hardly seemed likely that he would learn anything reassuring from my Colonel in Leicester. I realized that I should have to take a risk with him.

Looking him straight in the face I said sharply: "You are making a big mistake, sir. If you take my advice you will ring up the War Office and ask for Room 654. They will tell you all you need to know about me."

The success of this move depended upon his being a Regular. If he was, he would probably know what Room 654 meant.

He sat down, shuffled his papers and then came to a decision.

"I beg your pardon. You needn't say any more."

We shook hands and I thankfully left him.

Outside it was still pouring with rain and our poor old Dakota looked like a seedy goose which had taken its last emigrational flight. Some way down the road I saw a small car approaching, and as it drew near, one of the naval men said to the other, "I spy hostile craft to starboard."

Without a word, each of them grabbed his bulging case and vanished into the 'Gents'.

The car drew up and two Customs men got out. We lined up outside the stores and again we had our luggage examined. Of course none of us mentioned the Navy, and as our landing had been impromptu the Customs had no list of the passengers. I suppose our pilot had one, but I never saw him and I believe he was fast asleep. When they got to me they went quickly through my hold-all and asked me what I had in my parcel.

"Ah," I said, "this parcel is Top Secret. I had instructions not to undo the outer wrapping until I reached England. I was then to post it—to the War Office, I suppose."

"Well, sir," said one of the Customs men, "why not undo it now?"

Under the curious gaze of two pairs of eyes I ripped off the outer covering and read the lettering underneath. *To: Mrs. E. Matthews, 25 Dart Street, Swansea, South Wales. Contents: chocolates, soap, tinned fruit.*

Seeing my expression of disgust the Customs men roared with laughter, and when I told them the full story they thought it even funnier. Still laughing they drove away. I wondered if they would have laughed so much if they could have seen the two naval men emerge from the lavatory with their contraband intact.

Some little time later we were driven to a little railway station about fifteen miles from Exeter where we made for the office of the Railway Transport Officer.

The R.T.O., an elderly Captain, was sitting with his feet on the table picking winners for the day's races. Seeing us troop in he looked up from his paper and grunted "Yes?"

"We're a party of ten," I explained, "and we've just arrived by air from Egypt. May we have railway vouchers, please?"

Putting his feet down he surveyed us disdainfully.

"Certainly not. I know nothing about you. I have no orders to issue vouchers to a party of ten."

Replacing his feet and picking up his paper again, he added: "You'll have to pay your own fares. Good morning."

After all we had gone through this was a little too much. I was quickly thrust aside by one of the naval men.

"Listen, you old fool," he began, "we've been pushed around long enough this last day or two. You'll issue us with ten vouchers, do you hear?"

"Don't you talk to me like that," said the R.T.O., stuttering with rage. "I'm in charge here. Clear out, the lot of you!"

"Right, snapped the Navy, "you've asked for it. Come on, you chaps, let's wreck this lousy dump and chuck the old fool on the line."

"Coom on lads, oop the Durhams!" shouted Tweedledum.

The R.T.O. backed against the wall looking scared. "All right, all right, gentlemen, perhaps there's been a mistake," he quavered.

The ten of us stood grimly while he made out our vouchers, and I've never seen a man look more relieved than he was when we trooped out of his office. Our train soon came in and we reached Waterloo at about half-past ten that night.

CHAPTER XVIII

I ESCAPE ARREST AS A DESERTER

Next morning I reported to the War Office, and once again I walked down those familiar winding passages to Room 654. Entering, I found the same grey-haired lady sitting tapping away at her typewriter. Although a whole life-time had passed since last I had seen her, she nodded and smiled at me as if she had seen me only the day before.

In his room I saw Colonel Lester. He was wearing the same suit and looking exactly as he always looked.

Somehow I had been expecting a dramatic climax to my adventures, though I don't quite know what. Perhaps a crowd of people to congratulate me, or a severe ticking off for having failed in my duties. But I might have known that Colonel Lester would greet me as casually as if nothing had happened at all.

"Well, James," he said, stubbing out his cigarette. "So you got back safely?"

I suppressed a desire to ask him a whole string of questions.

"We thought of bringing you home aboard a destroyer," he went on, "but flying is quicker, I suppose."

Although he must have known that I was itching with curiosity to hear the worst, this maddening man then took a pencil from his pocket and began doodling.

At last he looked up and said quietly: "Thank you. You did a great job."

He grinned at me. "I sent a full report over to the P.M. I wrote it out like a film scenario. He was tickled to death with it, and also the way you carried it off."

Changing his tone he asked briskly: "What next? Would you like to transfer to a film unit, or have some leave?"

I was still too anxious to know what effect the Impersonation had had on the war effort to take much interest in such trivial matters. When I asked him, he took a couple of turns up and down the room before replying.

"From the reports which have come in the whole thing was a great success," he said.

This was a weight off my mind. Whatever happened now, I had not failed in the thing which really mattered. But for some reason making Army films which had seemed so thrilling only a short time ago had now lost all its attraction.

"If you can arrange it," I said, "I should like to return to my unit. I've had rather a nerve-racking time of it and I think my best plan is to get back to my job and try to forget it all."

He smiled a little grimly. "You may not realize it, but you have a pretty sticky time ahead of you. When you get back to your unit everyone will want to know what you've been doing and why your skin is tanned. Tell them any story you like, so long as it isn't the truth. You may think the need for secrecy is past. This is not so. You must still keep your mouth shut. Can I trust you to do that? On no account tell a soul what you've been doing."

"No, sir."

"Good. There's just one thing more. I think I should take you over to your G.O.C. Pay Corps and let you have a word with him. After that we must part."

As it turned out, I had good reason to be thankful to him for the chat I had with the General. Colonel Lester had warned me that a sticky time lay ahead of me but I doubt if he knew quite how sticky it was going to be.

All this time, remember, I had not been allowed to send a single word to Eve, who I thought must have given me up for lost by now. But on reaching London the night before I had phoned her in Leicester. Hearing my voice she had almost sobbed with relief and she began to bombard me with questions

N

which of course I could not answer. I had to tell her that I would not be able to see her for a day or two and that I must leave all news until then.

Sitting in a train on my way to Leicester I trembled to think of the double barrage of questions which would be laid on me—the first by Eve and the second by my brother officers. Once again I began trying to formulate watertight fibs which I would stick to no matter what happened.

Eve was waiting for me at the station. I doubt if a husband ever met his wife with such conflicting emotions.

Holding me at arms' length she began: "How brown your face is! Where have you been all this time? *Please* tell me."

"Not now, darling. Let's get home, then I'll tell you everything."

This gave me a little more time to put the finishing touches to the story I had concocted, and when we got there I told it with as great a show of conviction as I could muster.

At the last moment, I said, the hush-hush filming had been called for after all. Until it was finished I had been forbidden to say a word about it and the Special Pay Duties was just a blind.

The thing we had to film was the results of important tests carried out with certain new types of weapons. For greater secrecy these tests had been conducted in Africa. Professional actors had been needed for the job because in making the films we had had to give running commentaries on the technical details.

I must have been fairly convincing because this time she seemed to believe my story, though she said she couldn't understand why I had not written to her once all the time I had been away. I countered this by explaining that we had been forbidden to write to anyone at all for fear of our letters falling into enemy hands.

But to jump ahead of my story—a few weeks later I had rather a shock. Returning home one evening I found Eve sitting sewing. Without looking up she said, "You know the tobacconist's shop at the corner by the bus stop?"

"Yes."

"A funny thing happened today when I went in there and asked them the time——"

"How was it you didn't know the time?"

"Now you've made me forget what I was going to say. Oh yes—the man behind the counter said: 'Half-past eleven. I know my clock's right because I always check it when "Monty" passes to catch the 7.45 tram when he goes to the Pay Office every morning.' "

There was an awkward pause. "Well, dear," I said, "what's funny about that? I believe I'm supposed to be slightly like Monty."

"Yes, I know, but it's more than that. You've changed in a queer sort of way. Sometimes your whole manner is different and you've said some extraordinary things in your sleep."

This time she didn't ask me the usual question, but it was there just the same although unspoken. Was there always to be this mystery between us? I think I came nearer to telling her the truth that evening than ever before. Surely, I thought, there could be no harm in it now that the whole thing was over? And then I remembered Colonel Lester's warning and I said nothing.

Long afterwards Eve told me that she had half guessed the truth. She connected the photograph in the *News Chronicle* with my first interview in London and believed that I was 'working with General Montgomery', as she put it.

The morning after I returned to Leicester I walked into the Pay Office headquarters and went straight to the Adjutant's office where I found my old friend George Reid. Naturally I expected that he would be pleased to see me, but at once I was aware of a strained atmosphere.

"Hullo," he exclaimed, standing up. "So you're back? You look as if you had been sun-bathing in the South of France."

I grinned at him and shook my head.

"I'm not going to ask you where you've been," he went on, "or why you did this crazy disappearing act. But I warn you, you're for the high jump."

He looked at me as if expecting me to offer some explanation, but there was nothing I could say. Nor had I the despondent air of a deserter driven into returning and facing arrest. I think I must have been a profound puzzle to him.

"The Colonel has given me orders to take you straight in to him—if and when you come back. You'll have a good deal of explaining to do, I should say. Come on, let's get it over."

He marched out of the office and I followed him marvelling at his starchiness and formality.

Presently I found myself facing the Colonel with George standing stiffly to attention beside me. For some moments the Colonel did not speak. I suppose his feelings were too much for him. He just sat and stared at me with no very pleasant expression.

Looking back on it now I can sympathize with his indignation. Quite suddenly he had been told by his General that a junior officer of his to whom he had granted a week's unofficial leave on the plea that he was wanted for filming was removed from his Command for Special Pay Duties.

He must have known that this was a put-up job. In the first place, any officer chosen for Special Pay Duties would have to be a Regular and not inferior in rank to a Major, with years of experience behind him. Furthermore, this officer would be posted officially, his name appearing in Part I Orders, not to mention the circulation of a great many official memos.

He knew that sand had been thrown in his eyes, and not only was his pride hurt, but his years of Army training made him incensed at the apparently casual way I had walked out of the Pay Office and simply disappeared. As I looked at him I dimly guessed what was passing in his mind.

"Well, James," he began quietly, "so you have decided to return to your duty station? Some time ago you came to me with a cock-and-bull story about Army films and you showed me a letter from—a friend of yours, I have no doubt. On the strength of your story and the letter, and I may say against my better judgment, I granted you one week's leave. Is that correct?"

"Yes, sir."

"The General rang me up and informed me that you were to go on Special Pay Duties."

"Yes, sir."

Suddenly he lost control. "Damn it, man," he shouted, "you don't know the first thing about Special Pay Duties!"

Of course I couldn't deny that. More quietly he continued: "What sort of Special Pay Duties do you think you're capable of? The only kind that I know are investigating cases where there has been some grave deficiency in regimental or other funds."

He leaned back in his chair. "What were these Duties? Where have you been?"

All I could reply to this was that I had been severely cautioned to keep my mouth shut. Naturally this did not go down very well with him.

"Very well," he said, "I will tell you what I propose to do. I shall put you on a charge as a deserter. Perhaps we shall get at the truth about your movements when you come up before a court martial."

I stood there in front of him unable to say a word. And suddenly he exploded again.

"You, a junior officer, having the infernal audacity to try and put one over on your own Colonel! I don't know what you've been telling the G.O.C., but I am not deceived."

Turning to George he snapped, "Send in Major Walters."

I saw then that he meant business and that I should have to take a risk.

"May I speak to you privately, sir?" I asked.

"Very well," he growled. "Wait outside, Reid."

When the Adjutant had gone out I said, "I am very sorry to have to put you in this position, sir, but I am under strict orders not to say one word to anyone about what I have been doing."

He frowned at me and then began fuming. "Under *whose* orders? You are under *my* orders, aren't you? Who else can give you orders, I should like to know, without referring to me?"

There was no answer I could think of to this.

"Frankly, I don't believe a word of your story," he said, stretching out his hand to press the bell on his desk.

I knew then that I should have to break my promise to Colonel Lester and tell him whom I had been working under or else face arrest, court martial and Heaven knows how much unwelcome publicity and awkward cross-examination.

Psychologists can explain it how they will, but as I realize now, it was moments of danger or emergency which jerked me back into the Monty role. I heard myself saying in a cold, precise tone: "Pick up that phone and get on to the War Office—understand? Ask for MI 5. They will tell you all that it is necessary for you to know."

He looked at me in amazement, and without a word he picked up the receiver. But on second thoughts he replaced it, sighed deeply and gave me a sudden smile.

He said, "There was a rumour going round here that you were in the Tower of London waiting trial as a spy."

I couldn't help returning his smile.

"I am glad it was only a rumour," he went on drily, "both on your own account and on mine. I suppose you can't tell me anything—off the record?"

"I am very sorry, sir, but I have been given the strictest

instructions not to talk to anyone. The official story is that I have been on film work connected with Top Secret weapons." I grinned at him. "The Special Pay Duties wasn't a very good one."

To do him justice, he bore me no ill-will for keeping my lips sealed, and we parted on friendly terms.

"Very well," were his last words. "Report to your section and call Reid in."

I believe he was thinking that an officer of his being chosen to carry out Secret Service work was after all rather flattering to his battalion. As I went to the door he actually gave me a sly wink.

George was standing outside looking more than a little worried.

"Hullo, Georgie," I greeted him. "It's all over and the old man wants you."

He stared at me in great astonishment. "Isn't he going to put you on a charge?"

"Whatever for? I told him where I had been and everything's perfectly O.K. now."

Later on when he had been in to the Colonel I told him my story about filming secret weapons and I was thankful to find that he swallowed it.

"We've all been worrying about what was coming to you when you got back," he said darkly. Evidently the story about the Tower of London had been circulating pretty freely.

When I joined my section I soon realized that the men were bursting with curiosity to hear where I had been, so I told my Sergeant the hand-out story knowing that he would immediately repeat it in the Sergeants' Mess.

In the canteen questions were fired at me from all directions. Again and again I had to repeat my story, but not always with complete success. A few remained sceptical and suspicious.

One officer told me it had been reported on the highest level that I had been arrested as a spy, and he seemed indignant that

I was not still a prisoner in the Tower. This story was repeated to me many times, and to this day I have never discovered who started it.

I soon settled down once again to routine work which was about as strongly in contrast to the work I had just been doing as it is possible to imagine. I tried hard to forget the past, but I came to realize that my fellow officers had changed their attitude towards me. They avoided me, and when I joined a group of them I noticed that they stopped talking.

I tried to discover what was the matter, but I did not succeed. I suppose the explanation is that I had become a mystery man and they felt uncomfortable when I was about. Obviously some of them had never believed my story about the filming, and no doubt fresh stories to account for my absence were already in circulation behind my back.

As time went by I began to feel the strain of this barrier which had formed round me. Some of my fellow officers never gave up questioning me as if they hoped one day to catch me out. I don't know what their motive was, but I found it trying to be for ever on the defensive.

As soon as the war ended I applied to go on the Control Commission in order to escape from this perpetual inquisition, but my application was refused. I was thankful when at last my turn for demobilization came and I was able to return to civilian life.

CHAPTER XIX

THE AFTERMATH

Soon after the end of hostilities a good many war books began to appear on both sides of the Atlantic. I wrote to Colonel Lester to ask if I might publish my story of the Impersonation, but he replied sternly that I was still under the ban of secrecy. However, things were soon to take a dramatic turn.

One day I was told by a friend that my name had been mentioned rather unflatteringly in a book called *My Three Years with Eisenhower*, by an American named Captain Harry C. Butcher. The county library got me a copy of it. The passage which referred to me was a little surprising.

After giving a short account of the Impersonation, the author went on: 'Someone walked into S.H.A.E.F. and with his tongue in his cheek said that Monty's Double had been seen staggering about Gibraltar, drunk, smoking a large cigar. Monty, livid, rose to the bait and was going to send disciplinary cables.'

Not being accustomed to the American style of humour I was somewhat taken aback. At length I went to the War Office and asked them if anything could be done about it. I was told no, they were powerless to do anything, for Butcher was an American and he had left the country.

But once again it was Monty who came to my rescue. When he heard about the book he was furious, and he saw to it that I was given permission to write a short 'vetted' version of my adventures. After he had passed it personally it was published in the *Sunday Express*.

There was a sequel to this. Four years later the editor of the *News Review* rang me up to ask if I knew that Captain Butcher was coming over to attend a D-Day Remembrance service on the beaches of Normandy. According to the American Press he intended to visit Great Britain to see me and apologize for what he had said about me in the book.

A week later the *News Review* gave me a short write-up, quoting the American newspapers. But the whole thing was a wet squib. Butcher never saw me or wrote to me.

Unwittingly he did me rather a bad turn. For months I had to put up with such greetings as: "Hullo, Jimmy, fancy seeing you! I wish *I'd* had as good a time as you did in the war—taking off Monty and staggering about from bar to bar."

Some people took a grave view of it. One pompous acquaintance told me I ought to be ashamed of myself letting down my country and getting drunk in the uniform of a British General. Ah well, I dare say I helped to pay for the radio station which Butcher bought with the proceeds of his book.

One day coming out of an agent's office I ran into a friend who took me along to a bar and stood me a drink. An elderly man was standing by the bar counter.

"Hullo, Collins," said my friend. "Out of the Navy at last, are you? May I introduce Mr. Clifton James."

Automatically he held out his hand, then stared at me and withdrew it.

"Clifton James, did you say?"

"Yes."

Glaring at me he said: "I have a bone to pick with you. Early one morning in Gib., after I had been on duty all night, I had just got into bed when I was ordered to turn out on parade to welcome General Montgomery."

With immense solemnity he went on, "I have since learned that it was *not* General Montgomery who fetched me out of bed that morning, but a certain Lieutenant Clifton James."

At first I thought he was joking, but he looked so much like an angry turkey cock that I realized he must have been nursing a grudge against me for years.

"I was only obeying orders," I said mildly.

"Capering round the Middle East dolled up like a bloody General!" Collins growled. "I expect you had the time of your life."

As a result of the articles which appeared in the *Sunday Express* I became for a while almost front-page news. A great many newspapers and journals both at home and abroad published photos of me alongside Monty. I was invited to parties and asked to address many different kinds of gatherings and tell them as much as I was allowed to about my adventures.

With my name on everyone's tongue I thought this might be a good opportunity to get back on to the Stage. Full of optimism I went for an interview with a theatrical manager. He gave me a most effusive welcome.

"Clifton James! I'm delighted to see you. Good heavens, you're the living spit of him. It's amazing. Excuse me a moment."

In no time his office was full of people who stared at me as if I were a waxwork. After they had goggled at me for some time I ventured to say: "I'm trying to forget all this. I came here to get some work."

At once there was an awkward silence and I soon found myself alone with the manager again. Sitting at his desk he looked at me sadly.

"I'm sorry, old man, there's nothing doing. I daren't cast you for a part, you'd be too much of a disturbing influence. The audience wouldn't be interested in the show but only in having a look at Monty's Double. Sorry, but there it is."

This was something new in my experience. Usually an actor hopes at all costs to make a name for himself, to be a household word with the public. But now it seemed that fame could be of the wrong sort. Wherever I applied I was received effusively, congratulated and shown to a gaping staff, but as soon as I asked for a job I was shown to the door.

At last I was driven to try for crowd work in the film

studios. I managed to get a small contract, but I was soon
pounced upon by the publicity man and photographed with
Jack Warner, Kathleen Harrison and other stars in my uniform
and a beret.

There was something comical in what happened next,
though at the time it didn't strike me as very funny. Just when
I was growing desperate I had a letter from a stranger who said
that he had a tip-top business proposition to offer me. He wrote
from an address in Manchester, and with high hopes I replied
at once asking for details. Back came a letter saying that the
writer could offer me big money if I would appear in the
North, opening early in the summer.

By return I wrote again enquiring what was the town and
the theatre. I also asked for a contract to be sent which I
promised to sign immediately.

A week went by before the eagerly awaited reply came.
Tearing open the envelope I read the enclosed letter and hardly
knew whether to laugh or cry. It said that the writer had a good
'pitch' at Blackpool on the South shore and would like me to
appear in his side-show on a sharing basis! I was pretty desperate, but I hardly fancied appearing as Monty alongside
freaks and fat ladies for holiday-makers to gape on.

Then something rather unexpected happened. One day I
had a phone call from a Staff Colonel at the War Office who
told me that Field Marshal Montgomery had promised to take
part in a pageant at Chilham Castle in Kent, but at the last
moment finding himself unable to go he had said, "Ask James
to take my place."

When I went down to the Castle I found that I had to make
a dramatic appearance through a yew hedge as a climax to the
pageant. On the cue 'Yet lastly we produced a Churchill and a
Montgomery' I came out from my hiding place, passed between
a double file of soldiers representing the Kent Volunteers in
the days of Napoleon, and standing in the midst of them I gave
the famous Monty salute.

Only a few of the audience were in the know, and the roar of applause which went up showed that the majority took me for Monty himself.

One evening I was asked to give a talk to an ex-Servicemen's Association. After the talk I was introduced to a grave-looking man who might have been an undertaker but who, as I soon discovered, was an archaeologist recently returned from Egypt. Before long he was describing a portrait head which he had unearthed and which he considered nearly as fine as the famous obsidian portrait head of King Amenemhet III.

This led him to tell me of the plot to assassinate Amenemhet I, and how when his son, Senusert, became King before his death he advised him: "Be on your guard against subordinates. Trust not a brother, know not a friend, and make not for thyself intimates, for it profiteth nothing."

Something prompted me to ask if he had ever met another archaeologist, Professor Salvadore Cerrini.

He stared at me. "Did you know him?" he enquired.

"I met him once for a few minutes," I replied, wishing that I had not mentioned the subject.

"Where was that?"

At that time I was still under a ban of secrecy about many of the details of the Impersonation. I countered by asking him why he had used the word 'did'. Was the Professor dead?

"Yes," he said quietly. After a moment he added, "He died under mysterious circumstances."

Naturally I wanted to hear more. He told me that soon after the war ended the Professor had been engaged on excavating a tomb in the Valley of the Kings, and one morning had been discovered dead from a knife wound. How he had met his death or what was the murderer's motive was still a mystery.

"Do you think a curse had been laid on the tomb?" I asked.

"Impossible to say. Curses often were laid on the tombs of

the Egyptian rulers and some of them worked out in very curious ways."

I thought of King Amenemhet's warning to his son and of the report which Professor Cerrini must have put in about Monty's visit to North Africa, but I said nothing.

Once you have been involved in Secret Service work you can never quite escape from it. I found that this applied even to me.

Soon after I began work on this book I had a phone call from somebody who gave his name as Max Harris and described himself as a journalist. He asked me for an interview. This surprised me. I told him that I was no longer Press news; but he brushed this aside and said he would come down from London the next morning.

When he arrived he turned out to be a very ordinary-looking man of about forty with the glib flow of conversation which you often find in Press-men. I couldn't see why he should want to talk about the Impersonation so long after the event, but this is what we did. Presently he asked me if I had any written account of it which gave more details than had yet appeared in print. I explained that I was writing a book which was not yet available.

"What I am really interested in is the planning of the job," he said.

"Planning?"

"Yes, the inside details of how MI 5 planned the whole thing."

No one had ever asked me this question before. "I know nothing about the inner workings of MI5. I had nothing to do with the planning. I was only a pawn in the game."

"Yes, but surely you knew something about what was happening behind the scenes?"

"Why are you so anxious to know?"

He was full of reasons why. The reading public were intensely interested in the Secret Service. If I could tell him something about the way they went to work it would make a good story. He promised to go fifty-fifty with me on the proceeds of his writings.

It seemed plausible enough, but I could tell him nothing for the very good reason that I didn't know the answers. He continued to press me for details and at last I was thankful to get rid of him by giving him some notes of mine which really told him nothing.

A fortnight later there was a ring at the front door bell and there was Harris again without any warning of his coming. I didn't see how to avoid inviting him in and presently he was asking me if I had considered his proposition.

"What proposition?" I asked bluntly.

"Well, I'll put my cards on the table. If you will give me details of the planning, the full version of your assignment and the real names of the MI 5 people who briefed you—I'll make it worth your while. You see, I have a connection with a group of American newspapers, and between you and me, money is no object to them."

This certainly sounded an attractive offer and I admit that the thought crossed my mind that I might cash in on it. Naturally I couldn't tell him the truth, even if I had known it, but I supposed that neither the American reading public nor the American editors would be any the worse for a little fiction provided it sounded plausible and no one discovered that it was fiction. But my dreams of easy money were shattered by the arrival of my doctor, Bob Graham, who in my rickety state of health was a constant visitor. As usual he was breezy and cheerful, but when I introduced him to Harris his manner changed.

"Haven't we met before?" he asked.

I should mention that Bob had been in the Intelligence Service and had a keen memory for faces.

"No, I don't think so," Harris replied.

Bob shrugged his shoulders and begged to be excused while

he wrote me a prescription. I was not aware that I needed any prescription, and when he handed it to me I began to put it in my pocket.

"Read it," said Bob sharply.

In some surprise I glanced at it and read: "Get rid of this man at once. He's dangerous."

I think Harris must have guessed what was happening, for almost at once he left with an unconvincing promise to get in touch with me later.

When he had gone I asked Bob what he knew about him.

"Just one of those coincidences," he replied. "I ran across him in Belgium. He was working for us then, and as we discovered later for the other side as well. I expect he's still up to his tricks. What did he ask you?"

I dare say I shall be an object of mild interest to enemy agents until the end of my life.

THE END